ENDORSEMENTS

Morag Barrett has brilliantly put into words the complexities of the human factor at work! Almost everyone has people they love to work with . . . and people they most definitely do not. Cultivate *shows you how to develop a long-term focus and improve working relationships with everyone from the supporter to the rival and even–especially!–the adversary. An inspiring read!*
—Marshall Goldsmith, author of the *New York Times* and *Wall Street Journal* best seller *Triggers.*

How do you build effective working relationships in your organization? In this book, Morag Barrett draws on her extensive business experience to offer an insightful response to this fundamental question. Barrett helps us identify key relationships that merit our attention the most, as well as how to work effectively with allies, rivals, and adversaries.
—Michael Roberto, Trustee Professor of Management, Bryant University

Morag brings new ways of seeing workplace dynamics and success. The Relationship Ecosystem is a powerful approach to understanding critical stakeholder relationships, and how to move forward together.
—Shannon Sisler, SVP Talent Management, Western Union

Morag Barrett has hit a home run. She has challenged us all to embrace the most important verb in winning lasting and genuine relationships —Cultivate.
—Tommy Spaulding, *New York Times* bestselling author of *It's Not Just Who You Know*

We should never underestimate how much we depend on people to get things done in life and in business. The relationships we have and the ones we intentionally develop are often the ones that shape how we accomplish things in life. Cultivate *outlines how successful people and teams can create the relationships that have the most impact in their organizations.*
—Michael Dunn, Global CTO, Match

Cultivate *delivers engaging tools to navigate every dynamic relationship in your life. No more shying away from crucial conversations and hard issues!*
—L'Teisha Ryan, Director, Corporate
Communications, Ball Corporation

Cultivate. The Power of Winning Relationships *is a powerful tool for those seeking to navigate and grow relationships—in business and in life—and produce more, enjoy more and thrive!*
—Lida Citroen, Principal, LIDA360

I recently attended an Executive Boot camp created by Morag Barrett. The information is spot-on and delivered with a fantastic sense of humor. I recommend this book to anyone who wants to learn how to get their strategy adopted, supported, communicated, and executed.
—Richard Hanke, Executive Director
Global Healthcare Exchange

Morag is able to draw meaning around concepts we can sense to be true, but so often have a difficult time expressing and acting on in real time—until now!.
—Jose Acevedo, Technology & People Visionary, Topgolf

Morag has the unique insights and professional experience that are prerequisites for writing a book on cultivating and building strong relationships in and out of the work place. Those who read this book will profit by it.
—Dale Knipp, Vice President, Business
Development, CSG International

Cultivate *enables readers to identify key relationships and create a plan for moving them forward. It has been transformative in my business.*
—Chris Petrizzo, CLIQ Instructional & Performance Solutions

With a mind-shifting perspective on working relationships, Cultivate *will change the way you see and build intentional business allies.*
—Michael Turner, President & CEO, revgen partnerss

cultivate

THE POWER OF WINNING RELATIONSHIPS

MORAG BARRETT

GREENLEAF
BOOK GROUP PRESS

Published by Greenleaf Book Group Press
Austin, Texas
www.gbgpress.com

Distributed by Greenleaf Book Group

For ordering information or special discounts for bulk purchases, please contact Greenleaf Book Group at PO Box 91869, Austin, TX 78709, 512.891.6100.

Cataloging-in-Publication data is available.

Print ISBN: 978-1-62634-242-2

eBook ISBN: 978-1-62634-243-9

Part of the Tree Neutral® program, which offsets the number of trees consumed in the production and printing of this book by taking proactive steps, such as planting trees in direct proportion to the number of trees used: www.treeneutral.com

TreeNeutral

Printed in the United States of America on acid-free paper

15 16 17 18 19 20   10 9 8 7 6 5 4 3 2 1

Second Edition

For those friends, colleagues, clients, and seminar participants, in twenty countries on four continents, who have helped shaped me and this book, I thank you for your patience, insights, and encouragement.

The time has finally come to put my pen (or laptop) where my mouth is and get down to business.

Morag Barrett

Contents

Acknowledgments

This book may have one name on the cover, but it took an army to make it a reality. I want to share my heartfelt thanks and gratitude to everyone who has touched this project, however fleetingly. This was a marathon sprint that I couldn't have completed without you all cheering me on and helping me believe when I doubted.

To my Book Advisory Board, a team of volunteers who came together to hold me accountable and ensure I took action to write the book: Jose, Lauri, Cynthia, Dale, Chris, and L'Teisha. This was the most inspiring collaborative experience I have been part of. From the start you did not hold back, you shared your thoughts, what you liked, and candid feedback and suggestions to improve each chapter. Allies from the start and Courage & Vulnerability in action.

To Bradley Rood, Wendy Bohling, Ray Wilson, Ian Llewellyn-Nash, and Richard Hanke, who demonstrated Abundance & Generosity in sharing their feedback and personal stories of professional relationships at work.

To past and present members of SkyeTeam, Alexis, Lorna, Amy, and Jonathan, who helped shape my original thinking and workshop these concepts, and Eric, Corinna, and Lauri, my team of Allies. Go Unicorns!

To my family, Nick, James, Matthew, and Christopher, who have watched me spend hours writing and rewriting each chapter, and experienced the page by page drama that goes into writing a book. My brother, Andrew, who epitomizes the Ally Mindset towards all he meets. And finally to our parents, John and Lucy, who aren't here to see this book published, but who I know are watching from afar.

To all of you who have supported me on this journey, I thank you from the bottom of my heart.

I am your Ally.

FOREWORD

I'm humbled to be asked to write this foreword. *Cultivate: The Power of Winning Relationships* by Morag Barrett is a comprehensive tour of the most powerful insights about business relationships. We've heard many of them before, if not all in one place, but with this unique and clear perspective on why it matters: "Managers spend between 70% and 90% of their time working with others . . . a wasted opportunity if it is not coupled with deliberate attention to developing relationships." Morag builds on the teachings of relationship mavens and on her own experience coaching teams to define what that deliberate attention should be.

A survey of that much relationship landscape—from emotional intelligence to a nicely articulated view of my own generosity, intimacy, candor, and accountability mindsets with abundance as the frame for mutual success—could be dizzying in lesser hands. But Morag pulls it all together in a Relationship Ecosystem Model that helps the reader think about relationships in the context of both interpersonal skills and the broader dynamics of organizational culture.

The book gets very practical with Morag's *Speaking Up: Four Strategies*, a model for framing conversations designed to transform relationships. The reader comes away with the necessary tools for diagnosing relationship issues and fixing them with specific conversational practices. The result, once you make those practices your habit? Greater success for both you and your organization.

Using Morag's own terminology, some might think of us as Rivals, but we're natural Allies. I look forward to a discussion about how, together, we might help people cultivate relationships using her best practices on the front lines of business to drive even more success than this new book surely will.

Keith Ferrazzi, Author, *Who's Got Your Back* and
Never Eat Alone and CEO of PocketCoach, Inc.

Introduction

No man is an island entire of itself; every man is
a piece of the continent, a part of the main.

« John Donne »

My journey has been long and winding, with plenty of bumps in the road.

I was originally planning to become an engineer—studying physics, applied mathematics, and economics. However, those plans changed in my high school economics class, "How Banks Create Money." This resulted in a change in direction, and I joined one of the largest banks in the UK. My career for the next fourteen years was set. (By the way, banking is nothing like that chapter in economics!)

I thrived in the industry, reveling in the numbers and the predictability of ratios, analyzing the growth strategies for complex businesses, making recommendations, and approving million-pound loan applications. (Some of them seemed to *weigh* a million pounds, too.)

• • •

Keep Calm and Carry On.

• • •

This wasn't a time when much consideration was given to building relationships across the organization. We were still a traditional, command and control, rule-based environment. This didn't last, though. The early '90s was a time of sweeping change in the UK banking industry. Deregulation was increasing competition. Customers were demanding personal service, a relationship-based approach to banking, whether retail or corporate.

A focus on relationships, between employees and toward customers, could differentiate our bank from its competitors. And it did.

After leading those change efforts, which impacted both the organizational culture and our approach to clients, I chose to leave the relatively safe confines of the bank.

My next stop was the volatile telecom industry, in the midst of the dot-com bubble, as I joined an American firm that promptly exposed me to a global business environment.

Working relationships became even more complex when time, distance, and national culture were part of the equation. In this fast-paced startup environment, the value of relationships was high. But that didn't necessarily mean the business culture was healthy.

This opportunity ultimately brought me and my family to the United States, where we needed to build new relationships, both personal and professional, and a new support structure in a new country.

As I reflect back on my career, there are many colleagues I'd jump at the chance to work with again. They challenged me to exceed expectations—not just the expectations of others, but ones I had for myself. They provided "tough love" and feedback when I needed to hear it, and they were there by my side cheering me on in the good times. They were the individuals I could call upon in a time of need, and without hesitation they would do everything within their power to help. Those same people also knew they could call me in their time of need.

These were my allies.

On the other side of the coin were the colleagues who left a different impact. These individuals were examples of what *not* to do, the person *not* to bring onto the team, the person with whom you had to watch your back. When they left the organization, a collective sigh of relief was heard. These were adversaries. Thankfully, I can count my adversarial relationships on one hand.

A Toxic Waste

Early in my career, I experienced a toxic work environment—a boss who micromanaged and took credit for my work, along with a peer who was resentful of my promotion. Despite a number of measurable successes, my memory of this time is a lack of fulfillment. There were many days when I was close to quitting.

My friendly colleagues would ask, "How do you put up with it? They should do something!"

We knew something was wrong, but neither this mysterious "they" nor I had the perspective, tools, and approaches to tackle the situation. So instead, I did the "British" thing, keeping a stiff upper lip and working through it.

I epitomized the World War II meme Keep Calm and Carry On. In other words, I did nothing, I said nothing, and I hoped the quality of my work would somehow win out.

It did, but at some cost. I was stressed out, continuously looking over my shoulder, concerned about what might happen. What a waste of energy.

This experience also taught me that relationships at work are the key to our success and our well-being, and they are ultimately critical to the amount of enjoyment we get during office hours.

Yes, having fun and feeling satisfied with relationships at work are important! For many of us, the hours we spend at work far exceed the time we spend with our families or in social settings. So why not actually enjoy this massive part of our lives?

Working respectfully is not a win/lose power struggle. Nor is it "soft" to have a conversation about how you work together. When you cultivate winning relationships, everyone involved can benefit—especially you.

Bottom Line Metrics

My business successes aren't only measured in fun-metrics, but there are plenty of financial and competitive advantages to enjoying positive relationships at work—and there are also many real-world liabilities for toxic relationships.

Personally, my self-confidence faltered in negative environments. My focus moved from leading with my strengths to operating from a fear of failure. As I avoided risk and mistakes at each turn, my creativity faltered. I became reactive instead of proactive. I sought permission at each small step along the way, rather than taking the game-changing actions the new role required.

For the organization, the consequences included a slowing of information and decision-making, as my boss insisted upon being consulted on every decision. Others within the team hesitated to work with my boss for fear of coming into his crosshairs. Employees became disillusioned, engagement fell, and individuals (especially the high performers) chose to leave the organization.

In my banking career, I quickly realized that it was not enough to have a detailed business plan, an innovative product, or a leading edge service. To be successful, organizations also needed to focus on the *people* side of the business; ensuring that employees were working together to deliver on the business plan. We saw too many companies overlook this critical element, and as a result business floundered.

The business plan means nothing. You can have the shiniest new product, but if you don't get people aligned to execute the plan, you do not have a sustainable business. This is why I do what I do. This is why I wrote *Cultivate*. Relationships matter.

The reality is that any relationship—professional, social, or familial—has two participants. As the phrase goes, "It takes two to tango," and as a ballroom dancer I know this to be true! I owed it to my boss just as much as I did to myself to ask for what I needed. However difficult, I needed to find the opportunity and words to explain the impact of our working relationship on me, on my enthusiasm for her, and on my enthusiasm for the company.

But How?

Leaders and managers end up spending a disproportionate amount of time immersed in resolving interpersonal conflicts of one sort or another. In the best scenario, the relationships we encounter are those that leave us energized for the future—a group of engaged people working together rather than against each other.

Even when people focus on taking established relationships from "ground floor to C-Suite" they don't address those relationships that are already in the basement—because they simply don't know how to cultivate! Most leadership programs focus on the characteristics of high-performing teams and engaged employees but spend little time on the nuts and bolts of improving working relationships (which results in an exceptional organization). They don't provide insight into the symptoms of a healthy relationship or one that's deteriorating.

I've also come across frameworks that acknowledge the importance of relationship-building in the workplace; however, they seem to present relationships as a linear set of experiences—a *buy me flowers and I will fall in love with you* approach.

Relationships at work are not as neat and tidy as linear models may lead us to believe. Relationships are fluid by nature; people and relationships come and go. I wanted to understand why some stood the test of time and conflict while others crashed and burned or simply fizzled out.

There is no one single panacea that can guarantee success. While the concepts are simple, the strategies require discipline to implement and to operate consistently with the right mindset. We can all be great on our best days, but in times of uncertainty or turbulence, we may have a tendency to throw out the rule book and resort back to counterproductive behaviors.

Small World

If the world is small, the business world is microscopic. This fact should encourage you, but it may also scare the daylights out of you. Good news about your accomplishments will spread, but at nowhere near the pace of bad news. Your reputation precedes you, as the saying goes.

Let's look at the positive side. This story helps illustrate the smallness of planet earth. I was sitting at the Anchorage airport, having facilitated leadership programs at the North Slope, Alaska. (It's a long way from anywhere!) It was my first trip to Alaska, and I knew no one in Anchorage, let alone anyone sitting at the airport at four o'clock in the morning. The royal wedding was being broadcast on the screens in the terminal, and the lady next to me started to chat. Apparently I have an accent, and she wanted to talk about my life in England. It was early, and I wanted to see the dress before boarding, so we chatted. Eventually the conversation turned to current things. I shared that I lived in Colorado. She knew someone in Colorado . . . it turned out that her friend was someone I know well. We immediately went from strangers with nothing in common to acquaintances with someone in common.

This is just one of hundreds of chance encounters I have experienced in my travels around the world—encounters that only serve to reinforce that we are just one conversation away from reaching our dreams, or at least taking a step closer to them; that if we take the time to talk to those around us, we can cultivate relationships that result in a positive and lasting impact for all of us.

Theory Is Not Enough

This book provides insight and practical skills needed to cultivate winning relationships. What follows is the culmination of over twenty years' personal experience of work, building business relationships, and helping others through the good, the bad, and the ugly.

I've made my own share of mistakes when it comes to professional relationships in the workplace: self-confidence interpreted as arrogance, a fear of having the tough conversations, and of not providing others with the feedback they needed to hear to ensure their success. I also have my share of success stories and relationships that have flourished. In doing so, we've enabled each other to be our better selves, achieve success, and celebrate accomplishments.

I've had the opportunity to facilitate hundreds of leadership programs, workshops, and executive coaching programs with organizations across the globe (more than three thousand leaders, in twenty countries, on four continents), from startups to Fortune 100 companies.

It is possible to build an ecosystem of positive relationships that will transform your career and the careers of those around you. I promise you this is more than a "be nice to each other" message. We'll go deep into people-science, and deep into how you relate to others, before digging into some very practical application.

Transforming your business relationships, and workplace culture, takes a personal commitment. But as you grow, you'll reap the rewards on a daily basis!

CHAPTER 1

the people side of business

Lots of people want to ride with you in the limo,
but what you want is someone who will take the
bus with you when the limo breaks down.

« OPRAH WINFREY »

We've all worked with people we find irritating: the person with an ego so huge the office has to install double doors to accommodate his or her super-sized head; the colleague who just can't stop talking about anything but work; or the poor soul who's desperate to share complaints every day.

One approach might be to avoid these people at all costs, but what if they're your boss or your peer? You'll need to spend a considerable amount of time in meetings with them, or working side-by-side, and your success will be intertwined with theirs.

Working with people who drive you nuts is exhausting and can, unfortunately, impact your attitude and performance. Emotions are infectious. Relationships are emotional.

Think about it. Have you ever walked into a room and just sensed, without talking to anyone, that something was up? Our emotional intelligence enables us to pick up on these clues, discriminate between them, and use this information to inform our thinking and actions to impact our behavior.

Being the smartest person in the room (IQ) is no longer (and may never have been) enough to ensure long-term success; technical skills and knowledge only contribute part of the equation. Emotional intelligence (EQ or EI), or people skills, is as important, if not more so, than IQ.

Emotional intelligence is the capacity for effectively recognizing and managing our own emotions and those of others. We can either leverage emotions to make the most of our important business and personal relationships or ignore them with potentially damaging results. In his book *Working with Emotional Intelligence,* Daniel Goleman[1] discusses four emotional intelligence skills, grouped under two main categories: personal competence and social competence.

Personal competence includes the following qualities:
- Self-awareness—how accurately you can identify *your* emotions in the moment and understand your tendencies across time and situation.

- Self-management—how you use awareness of your emotions to create the behavior that you want.

Once you have begun to master yourself, you can then move on to the qualities of social competence:
- Social awareness—how well you read the emotions of *other* people.
- Relationship management—how you use the first three emotional intelligence skills to manage your interactions with other people.

When I am working with teams, I will ask participants to identify three colleagues, bosses, peers, or subordinates, they would jump at the chance to work with again. We then explore what made these people memorable. Certain characteristics are mentioned again and again:
- They saw me as an individual; they cared about me.
- They connected with me as a person.
- They made time for me and listened to my ideas and suggestions.
- They gave me constructive feedback.
- They made me feel valued.
- They challenged me to deliver outstanding results.

What stands out is that the majority of the qualities are interpersonal—about *how* the person interacted with them, as well as the values he or she demonstrated. While we may recall how smart someone was, what people remember is the ability to connect with someone as a person, as a human being, and not simply as an employee, functional expert, or vendor.

If It Ain't Broke
Many of us understand the philosophical importance of relationships but struggle to put that understanding into action. I get plenty of agreement with these early concepts. However, when I ask, "How much time are you investing in cultivating winning relationships?" very few can say they devote deliberate effort.

Relationships are assumed to be effective until proven otherwise. Neutral relationships are valued as positive, when in fact the opposite is true.

Focus is on the task at hand, the "what needs to be done," and little or no time is devoted to the people side of "*how* we will get the task done." Success is measured in terms of individual results and individual contribution. Unfortunately, this approach actually sabotages our business goals!

The "me first" attitude is not surprising when you consider that our educational system reinforces this mindset. From the time you begin school, all the way through high school and college, there's a focus on graduating in the top X percent of your class by outperforming enough of your classmates. It's all about individual effort, and ultimately, individual success. Even where group projects are assigned, there is little time devoted to teaching effective team collaboration. So few have been taught the skills needed to work well with others, to hear alternative points of view, and to discuss differing viewpoints to increase understanding.

When we move from school to the workplace, this individualistic approach continues. We spend most of our time early in our careers developing our technical expertise, which is typically how we (and others) assess our value within an organization. As you progress through your career, the quality of your relationships has a greater impact on your success than your individual accomplishments. The ability to achieve results *with* others is your most valuable skill.

An inability to work well with others invariably leads to the stalling of careers or, even worse, implosion. An inability to "play well with others" will damage your reputation and long-term career success, no matter how many letters you have after your name, how many years of experience you have, or what your title is.

Organizations are full of examples of people who were technically competent and thus promoted up the ladder to manage others. Many times, these individuals are not provided with coaching, support, or training to understand that managing others requires a whole new set of skills—and a new mindset! As a result of this "sink or swim" approach to leadership development, many of these individuals self-destruct. No one wanted them on the team, or they were so quiet that no one recognized the value of what they brought to the table. This is an example of the "Peter Principle" or "Sheldon Syndrome"—a high IQ with low emotional intelligence.

Book Smart not People Smart

Mark was used to being the smartest guy in the room. He was always quick to volunteer his opinion, first to speak, and kept talking, dominating the conversation. Meetings with his peers were tense, and projects were not running smoothly. Instead of being a go-to guy, he was a *go-from* guy.

Mark was oblivious to this. He relished the "smart" image he had built up. After all, his technical knowledge brought him the promotion to head of his department. His promotion finally revealed what his team knew: he delivered results . . . alone, at the cost of relationships across the company and within his department.

Mark had known things were tense, he hadn't realized that he was the problem. As our team shared the framework for identifying and cultivating relationships, he realized his intentions and actions were way out of sync.

Through coaching, we explored ways for Mark to adjust his behavior and approach—asking questions vs. telling, allowing others to talk first before offering his opinion, spending time getting to know his critical stakeholders, and asking them what they needed from him to help them be successful.

It was a rapid transformation. Relationships became more open and trusting. Mark's mid-year review evaluation was the best he had ever received. A 360 Feedback report completed during his coaching confirmed the change in approach was reaping benefits, not just for Mark but for his colleagues too.

One peer said, "He's so much more approachable . . . he listens to others' views . . . I feel more able to collaborate and work with him."

Why Fail?

Few leaders fail because of a lack of technical ability. Leaders fail because they do not cultivate effective working relationships across the organization. They do not have the ability to influence others to get results.

Think back through your own career, as you watched others rise or fail. When careers derail, it's not usually about expertise; it's usually because of mismanaged relationships. Let's be clear: knowledge of your

industry is important and critical to your ability to talk credibly, anticipate problems, and contribute effectively to discussions. However, these
skills are the minimum entry-level requirement that gets you a seat at the
table. Your ability to build and maintain high-quality relationships will
grow your success, and your team's success, to the next level of performance. This is *the* game changer that will accelerate your success. You
deserve to invest here!

Interestingly enough, even when formal leadership development is
provided, the results are not always beneficial. The American Society
of Training and Development's 2012 industry report indicated that American
businesses alone spent a staggering $156 billion on employee learning and
development. This is a phenomenal investment, especially when reports
go on to suggest that nearly two-thirds of organizations report that senior
managers are deficient in management and leadership skills and even more indicate that line managers and supervisors lack these skills[2].

> • • •
>
> *Managers spend between 70 and 90 percent of their time working with others . . . a wasted opportunity if it is not coupled with deliberate attention to developing relationships.*
>
> • • •

We teach people how to delegate,
project manage, and give annual reviews,
but we don't teach people how to intentionally improve working relationships.

According to John Kotter, the average (general) manager spends
approximately 25 percent of his or her time working alone. Most spend
between 70 and 90 percent of their time working with others, whether
attending meetings, ad hoc gatherings, or formal employee gatherings, or
responding to individual questions and requests for help.[3]

This is reaffirmed in the work I do with senior leaders and teams; all
this interaction is a wasted opportunity without deliberate and focused
attention on developing effective working relationships.

In an attempt to manage schedules and the numerous demands on
a leader's time, most meetings and interactions become purely transactional processes, destined to be average and deliver average results.

Whether you are a senior leader in an organization or an individual contributor, most professional relationships fail to move beyond this mechanical arrangement. It seems to be easier that way. It's about, "How can you help me in my current role or project?" with little attention focused on getting to know the other person, or how we can help them.

This is a shortsighted approach. To cultivate a winning relationship means that we take each relationship to the next level and build a personal connection, seeking to understand what motivates the person, what fears may be holding them back, how our individual styles are similar or different, and the implications for working together to deliver an outstanding result. Without this personal connection, collaboration, candor, and healthy competition are stifled. Shared learning and warnings of impending disaster are also curtailed, and competition potentially becomes destructive. Business relationships determine business success.

Social Workplace Bonds

In an article, the *Harvard Business Review*[4] found that social bonds were the major predictor of team success. The other two were "initiatives to strengthen relationships" and "leaders who invest the time to build strong relationships with their teams."

If team success (and individual success) is dependent upon social bonds, then it would follow that spending time getting to know the team members and articulating the rules of engagement for the team would be a good investment of time, right?

Creating these social bonds is much easier said than done. With the advancement in technology, email has become ubiquitous, to the point of actually undermining performance!

In a recent program presented by my team, leaders reported they each received several hundred emails a day. While email may be keeping leaders tied to their desktops, or with their smartphones permanently available twenty-four hours a day, it is also preventing the creation of meaningful connections and relationships at work.

I've experienced this in a large telecommunications firm, where an egalitarian approach backfired. We were a company of cubicles. You could walk corridors but not see anyone. People used email to chat with team members twenty feet away, and we wondered why there wasn't a real bond!

Contrast this with a working environment that was completely open: no walls, no hiding, and no excuses. Team members could simply raise their heads and talk to the person next to them. It led to a much different environment, where camaraderie and team relationships flourished. Don't get me wrong, we still needed "quiet time" away from the hubbub of the office and a private office to hold confidential conversations when needed. I am not suggesting you start knocking down walls to build relationships (although now that I think of it—yes I am—the metaphorical walls that prevent us from getting to know the person in the next office). My experience in both of these environments shaped my credo: "Get off your butt and go talk to someone!"

Even when teams get together to plan how they'll achieve a goal, many times they simply go through the motions of creating working agreements, clarifying goals and roles, only to promptly ignore them when they get back to their desks. Time is of the essence (emails continue to demand attention). And the perception that building relationships is "soft and fluffy" leads us to undervalue the time to focus on the interpersonal side of business.

I remember being told early in my finance career, "This is a business; there is no place here for emotions or personal connections." With such a philosophy it's little wonder that trust within teams declined and the confidence in the team leader was diminished. We all know when the rules of engagement have been broken. We sit in meetings drumming our fingers, clenching our teeth in frustration. We vent to our families and friends, but we remain silent at work.

We don't air our concerns for fear of the repercussions, or for fear of making an already stressful situation worse. We justify and excuse the situation because no one else is speaking up. We believe it is the way it has to be, and we don't want to go against the grain. We avoid the tough conversation with the very people who could effect change—our colleagues—and even ourselves.

Invariably, the inability to "talk it out" causes the situation to worsen until the relationship is so damaged there is little hope for reconciliation, at which point one or both parties leave the organization. You've seen it happen—perhaps in your own career.

Rules of Engagement

Asking for what you need to be successful at the start of each relationship or project (or renegotiating your needs for existing relationships) means you can more easily course correct when things go off track. Notice I said *when*, and not *if*! A proactive approach is the only option.

I've had the opportunity to work for managers (and with colleagues) who assumed I could read their minds, only to have them come down on me like a ton of bricks when my sixth sense fizzled. And I've been guilty of this myself.

Early in my banking career, there was lots of travel. On one occasion, my itinerary took me near the home of my parents, so I decided to stay overnight there rather than make the hundred-mile round trip required to return the next day. My boss didn't trust her team, and she made a habit of checking up on us. It got to the point where I would arrive at a branch and the manager would laugh and let me know that my boss had checked in on me already. On this occasion, my phone rang just as I arrived at my parents' house, an hour before the end of the workday.

"Where are you?" asked the prosecution. I gave an update of my activities and added, "I am staying overnight with my parents, and I'm reading some of the latest business books on—"

"That's not your job!" my boss barked.

Message received. I was stunned and burst into tears soon as soon as I hung up the phone. I remember discussing the situation with my dad, seeking his advice on what to do next. Together we talked through the options, how to start the conversation to bring positive change in the working relationship. I may not have realized it then, but it was another pivotal moment in writing this book.

This phone call was a prime example of not setting expectations. We didn't keep each other in the loop. Telepathy doesn't work and thinking it does is a recipe for disappointment. Far better to have a conversation that ensures we understand the expectations we have of each other, making the implicit explicit. Articulating the rules of engagement sets you up for success, both on the good days when things are going well and, more importantly, during the turbulent times when many of us revert back to inappropriate behaviors (micromanaging, command and control, or passive-aggressiveness, to name a few).

Rules of engagement could include the following steps:
- Ensuring that the two parties are in agreement regarding the objectives to be achieved.
- Agreeing on the levels of authority and decision-making responsibilities.
- Articulating roles and responsibilities.
- Understanding individual personality, communication, and decision-making styles, where these are in alignment and where they may be different, and the implications for *how* values and behaviors will be important to success.
- Meeting cadence—where and how often will meetings occur?
- Escalation process—when and who to ask for help and provide warnings of impending disaster.
- Feedback and coaching expectations.

Try these for your next project. By learning to set expectations, you find clarity about who you can rely on for advice and who can be a filter for tough decisions. Your team will also know who can be called on when you don't know how to solve a problem.

Old Enough to Know Better

An assumption that gets organizations and individuals into trouble is a false sense of security around age, tenure, or seniority. Too often I hear, "You've been in this industry long enough, you know what the priority is," or "I don't need to tell you how to do your job." This is particularly prevalent when experienced leaders join a new company. Rather than invest the time to effectively "onboard" a senior leader, many times the new team or organization takes a laissez-faire approach. While these seasoned senior leaders may have known what to do and how to do it at their previous company, the new company is a whole new ballgame, with a whole new set of players and a different culture.

I have no doubt that these experienced senior leaders will eventually work out the new rules of the game, but at what cost?

Having a conversation about WHAT needs to be done (the goals and objectives) is just one part of the equation. If you are not discussing the HOW of your working relationships, be prepared for the predictable surprise when things don't go as planned.

We need to care about others' success from day one. No matter how successful you've been, when you are working with a new team member, new team, or a new company, a candid conversation about the HOW is not optional for success.

You directly own the HOW. You conduct yourself and your interactions with others. Your reputation, your results, and your legacy depend on this.

In *The First 90 Days,*[5] author Michael Watkins shares that more than 40 percent of senior outside hires fail to achieve the desired results in the first eighteen months after transitioning to a new organization. Not only do these leaders fail, but he estimates that the number of people whose performance is compromised by the arrival of a new leader is 12.4 people. The estimated impact of the cost to a business of *one* failed senior hire is $2.7 million! Watkins gives three reasons for the high failure rate of outside hires:

- Not being as familiar with the organizational structure and the existence of informal networks of information and communication.
- Not being familiar with the corporate culture.
- Not being known to others in the organization and therefore not having the credibility of someone internal.

• • •

No matter how senior you are or successful you have been . . . you had better sit down and have a candid conversation . . . not just about the goals to be achieved but also around style and how things will get done.

• • •

These reasons are all directly related to relationships in the workplace. Failure isn't about "not being smart enough." It's all about the rules of engagement.

Every Day not Someday

How do you stay on top of the shifting landscape of working relationships? I would suggest you pause at least every three months to assess and reassess your personal and corporate landscape. In doing so, you will identify what has stayed the same, what has changed, and how this may have influenced your critical relationships. In addition to this good habit, the transition points listed below are opportunities to reevaluate your critical stakeholders:

- Promotion to a new leadership level.
- Transitioning into a new role or company.
- Challenged with delivering a business-critical, high-stakes goal at which you cannot afford to fail.
- A transfer to a new location, city, state, or country.
- Taking on a new project on which you are not the subject matter expert.
- Receiving feedback that you need to learn or develop a particular skill or competency.
- Going through a major organizational change or reorganization.

Who Knows You?

Cultivating winning relationships isn't just about getting business results today; it's also about the quality of your working relationships and your network as a whole. Are you on a path to deliver long-term success in your career aspirations? As has always been the case, the "who knows you" trumps "who you know." In today's hyper-connected world, this is even more pertinent!

With LinkedIn, you are only a few degrees removed from a hiring manager. Trust me; the savvy recruiters are reaching out to your connections for their perspective. This is more than collecting business cards, Facebook "Likes," or LinkedIn connections. It's about being thoughtful in developing your brand.

Whether you are using social media to build connections within your organization, or your company utilizes a similar tool as a company directory, having virtual connections does not equal having effective working relationships. To cultivate winning relationships, you need to get to know the person behind the online account.

Your success depends on it.

RELATIONSHIP REVELATIONS

- Few leaders fail because of a lack of technical ability. Leaders fail and careers flounder when we do not invest the time to cultivate effective working relationships.
- HOW things get done is as important as WHAT gets done.
- Cultivating winning relationships should be an ongoing, everyday habit.

YOUR RELATIONSHIP RESPONSIBILITY

Identify three people who have had an impact on who you are today and who helped you get to where you are today. Write their names below:

1. _____

2. _____

3. _____

What did these leaders/colleagues/people do? What characteristics did they demonstrate to make it onto this list? Write those characteristics below:

What did you learn from their advice or approach?

Relationship Challenge

To the extent you are able, contact the three people on this list and thank them for the impact they had on you.

For more practical resources, go to www.CultivateTheBook.com.

identifying your critical relationships

Managers learn in business school that relationships are either up or down, but the most important relationships today are sideways. If there is one thing that most of the people I know in management have to learn, it is how to handle relationships where there is no authority and no orders.

« PETER DRUCKER »

Who do you depend on for your success?

When I work with leadership groups, I sometimes use the analogy of a hamster wheel to talk about focus. For most of us, this means we're so busy running on our individual hamster wheels we forget to pause long enough to ask if we are running efficiently, or even running with the team!

Where back-to-back meetings are the norm and triple-booked requests for input clamor for your attention, is it any wonder I consistently hear managers say: *"I don't have time to think, let alone build relationships with other people . . . I need to keep ahead of my inbox and to-do list!"*?

Care and feeding of critical relationships means that you must find a way to stop and consider
- who (and what) may be helping and contributing to your success;
- who (and what) may be getting in the way of your success; and
- what action you need to take to continue to strengthen your workplace relationships and build on that success.

What Is a Critical Relationship?
Later in this chapter we'll shine a spotlight on your critical relationships, which may include:
- Your immediate manager or direct reports.
- Colleagues and team members with whom you work up, down, and across the organization.
- Those who have subject matter expertise and on whom you rely for advice.
- Those "upstream" of you who provide their finished work product, which then acts as the input for your own work.
- Those "downstream" of you and to whom you pass your finished work.
- Those who can provide warnings of impending disaster and the critical feedback needed to ensure that you stay on course.

Critical relationships are not just internal to your organization. They can also include customers, external organizations, vendors or other partners, and community organizations. Critical relationships can also include your family and friends.

One of my dearest and most important relationships is the one I share with my local barista. I'm not kidding. With a knowing glance, my triple-shot, extra-hot, no whip, mocha is under way—sometimes before I even make my way to the counter!

I also use the term *stakeholder* to further refine our critical relationships. A stakeholder is a more immediate professional relationship, one that has a direct impact on your success. An ineffective relationship with these stakeholders is likely to have more impact on your success than on theirs.

Let's discuss the three underlying premises to cultivating winning relationships.

Premise #1: The world of work is a team sport.

The world of work is likely the toughest team sport any of us will ever play. This is true whether you are working for a large multinational, a small startup, or a nonprofit. However, few of us are equipped with a mindset that values mutual success as highly as individual success.

Most arrive in the workplace well-schooled in the art of the solo game: "me vs. the exam board." It's all about individual effort, with little focus on how to achieve results with others. I liken it to the game of badminton (singles—which I used to play in high school), where success is about how fast we can return the shuttlecock at ever-increasing rates.

When we translate this to the workplace we see silos created where one individual, team, or department is pitted against another; where resources are used inefficiently; and where individuals no longer play to their strengths, but rather play to avoid a poor result. E-mails fly back and forth, until a winner and loser are declared.

Contrast this with a team sport like soccer, where each player is able to play to his or her individual strengths and yet is aware of the complete game as it unfolds. Players step in to provide backup and support to other team members as appropriate, falling back to their original position once that support has been provided. Scoring a goal can be achieved by one, but in most cases it is a result of passing the ball around and trusting others. The glory of winning (even the agony of defeat) is shared together, as an opportunity for the team to grow.

Even in a sole proprietor's enterprise, results are achieved through relationships with clients and other partners—work is a team sport.

Knowing that teamwork is important is a far cry from being an effective team player. What game does your organization play? What game are you playing? Or are you a spectator? Taking the time to identify your critical relationships allows you to maximize your potential and the potential of others.

Consider for a moment the results you are expected to deliver at work. My guess is that there will be very few, if any, that you can deliver independently of others in the organization.

Premise #2: You are dependent upon others for your success.

Take a moment and read that again . . . do you believe it? If work is a team sport, then you are dependent upon others for your success. You cannot perform at a high level alone. However, in many organizations a "hero mentality" abounds in which individuals wait to step in and save the day. In those organizations, I tend to see a short-term focus in which firefighting becomes the norm and long-range fire prevention is overlooked. In extreme situations, it's not just firefighting that occurs, but arson, where individuals actually *create* a crisis in order to be the hero. Those who save the day are then rewarded with other "problem areas to fix" or other recognition that serves to perpetuate the individual mindset. A culture of silos and barriers to collective success abounds!

• • •

. . . short-term focus where firefighting becomes the norm and fire prevention tactics are overlooked. In extreme situations it's not just firefighting . . . it's arson.

• • •

While this solo mindset may deliver results in the short term, burnout occurs when the self-imposed demands become too great. Team members may become complacent, sitting back and saying to themselves, "Why bother? She will just do it herself anyway."

For the organization, when key individuals leave, the institutional knowledge leaves with them. The lack of collaboration results in single points of failure that undermine corporate success.

Premise #3: Relationships matter.

We all prove our belief in this premise by our actions and our calendar. In order to succeed, you have to ask the following questions:

- How much time and energy am I investing in developing lasting business relationships?
- Am I thoughtful about which relationships are most important to my success?
- Am I proactive in building and maintaining my business relationships?

When my team works with leaders, we conduct an informal survey to find out how deliberate they are in cultivating relationships. We ask participants to raise their hands if they:

1. Use relationship management concepts and tools all of the time and could teach them to others.
2. Acknowledge the importance of relationship management but just don't seem to have the time to do it as much as they should or could.
3. Have thought about it but don't know how to implement the ideas.
4. Have never thought about the importance of cultivating winning relationships.

Less than a quarter of participants will raise their hands to the first statement. By far the vast majority of participants will acknowledge that they know it is important, yet they don't take the time or don't know how to put this into practice.

The How of Achieving Goals

Each year, organizations spend thousands of hours defining WHAT needs to be achieved in the near future—objectives are set, plans are made, Gantt charts are drafted, and to-do lists are created—all of which are tactical in nature. However, organizations nearly always overlook the HOW of achieving their goals:

- HOW we will behave when working together
- HOW we will talk about each other, especially when the other person is not present

- HOW we will resolve disagreements and respond when things do not go to plan
- HOW we will leverage our individual experiences and skills to work together to achieve the corporate goals

The HOW focuses on identifying who is involved in achieving each goal. Regularly reviewing this means we can identify new skills or capabilities that may be required and then determine how the organization will provide these, whether it will be an in-house (build) or a recruit-and-hire externally (buy) approach. In focusing on the HOW, an organization can identify new roles or additional headcount needed to support a growth strategy. It can look for opportunities to streamline and create efficiencies.

Unhealthy Care

A small health care company contacted us to work as an executive coach with one of its senior leaders, Stephanie. She was a high performer in many ways: she exceeded her sales targets, she was innovative, and her approaches to building a new client base were creative. She was focused, driven, almost obsessive when working on something that caught her attention.

This dedication was also apparent outside of work. Stephanie was a long distance runner who trained for hours a day, several days a week, to prepare for races across Europe. However, her husband and children were not receiving the attention they wanted or needed, and even the company leaders were concerned about the perceived lack of work-life balance.

We looked at WHAT was being achieved at work and explored HOW those results were being achieved. The goal was to balance working relationships for both short-term and long-term success.

We began with an awareness of important relationships and how Stephanie contributed to them. She had a conversation with each of her key stakeholders, both at work with her team and at home, that focused on what was important for them, how they defined success, and how they could work together to achieve it. At home the tactics started small: Stephanie began switching off the phone for a couple of hours in the evening; planning quality time with the kids; and taking her husband on business trips when possible and planning extra time for them to spend together. At work, it was about re-establishing the rules of engagement: who was responsible for what; empowering the team to make decisions;

clearly delegating projects; and assigning responsibility for achieving goals and milestones.

Over time it became apparent that things were moving in the right direction. Stephanie was less stressed at work. Her performance didn't suffer; in fact, colleagues commented that she was less prone to snap back at her team. Collaboration improved to the extent that a solution for a business problem that had remained unsolved for some time was found. At home, she found her running improved and the family was more involved together.

Avoiding the critical nature of the HOW conversations can result in the "we have always done it this way" mindset. Despite the allure of high performers and short-term successes, in the long term a focus on the WHAT only promotes average performance. We allow roles and responsibilities to remain implicit; we don't reset expectations regarding what success looks like. As a result, critical decisions can linger, allowing a product or service that's beyond its shelf life to continue to take energy away from what is truly important. Creating a culture of candor is what truly differentiates an average team from a high-performing team.

The Political Point of View

I recently had the opportunity to speak at a major conference attended by political leaders and staff from around the world. In an environment that actively encourages an adversary mindset, I was curious (and a little nervous) to see the reaction to these ideals.

There was overwhelming agreement that the concepts not only made sense but may be even more critical in a political environment.

The attendees recognized that at some point in their careers they would need the support of someone from "the other side of the house" to vote in favor of their initiative. Cultivating winning relationships before that vote is needed was critical. They recognized that finding a way to work respectfully, even if they disagreed with the political point of view, would actually benefit all.

Your Relationship Map

Let's hear from John Donne again and see if we're making progress: "No man is an island entire of itself."

As much as your ego may lull you into believing you have complete control over your own success, it's simply not true. We are all dependent on others, and it behooves us to remember this in all that we do. Every interaction, conversation, and relationship is an opportunity to help yourself by helping others.

Take a moment now and think about the three most critical goals or projects that you need to achieve in the next few months. Who is key to your ability to deliver those results or could prevent you from achieving those goals? My guess is that you quickly came up with a list into double digits. Don't lose this list . . . you will need it at the end of this chapter.

If you are dependent on others for your success, it's clearly in your best interest to help ensure their success. If your boss is successful, won't you be more successful? If your peers are succeeding, won't this have an impact on your success as well? If you manage people, isn't it your job to make them successful so you can also succeed? Conversely, if any of them fail, isn't there a strong likelihood that their failure will cause you to fail as well?

Here's a two-dimensional, simplified map of the connections you have. While you may be at the center of your map, recognize that each person you identify is also at the center of their own little universe. The ripple effects are mind-boggling!

Figure 1: Relationship Map

In most organizations, we see processes to obtain customer feedback, track on-time deliveries, and maintain quality controls, ensuring external perspectives are taken into account. While these are no doubt critical to our success, this narrow focus tends to overlook those who work immediately alongside us—our peers. Let's face it: a conversation about metrics is easier than a discussion about improving a working relationship!

When I present the relationship map in my programs, we have a discussion about who has the greatest potential to impact, and potentially undermine, your success. Time and time again, it is the examples of these relationships gone wrong that proves people are more often undermined by their peers than by any other stakeholder group.

Peers are in competition with us—not just for the next promotion or pay raise, but for limited company resources (budget, time with the bosses, and so on). This reality can lead to behaviors focused on "self," or individual success, and not on what is best for the business and our peers. Selfish attitudes between peers invariably result in damaged relationships, diminished reputations, and loss of confidence.

I worked with an organization where there were two senior leaders, one who looked after new product development and the other who led the operations team. Both were in dispute over who should receive an additional budget to fund their respective projects. They were focused on a "my group" approach, in which one would win and the other lose.

When the budget was allocated to the new product team over the operations team, the relationship between the two leaders deteriorated further. Others could see this—it impacted people's behavior and they avoided going to meetings and sharing information. They had to choose sides. Ultimately, the new product launch was unsuccessful, because operations personnel weren't engaged to make sure the implementation was effective.

Who won in this scenario? No one! Reputations were tarnished and the business impacted. Not because these two weren't smart enough, but because there wasn't a focus on the impact of their relationship.

We run the greatest risk of peers (or any stakeholders) undermining us when we are not being mutually supportive. It's a very different way of seeing your role within the organization.

In identifying stakeholders, we need to think about several questions:

- What are their goals and priorities?
- What would be the impact if I, or they, were to succeed or fail?
- What do I need from them? What do they need from me?
- How can they support/hinder/prevent me from achieving my goals?
- How do I feel about this person?

The Social Network

In creating your relationship map, don't just select "the usual suspects" and rely on the formal organization chart. When identifying your critical stakeholder relationships, also consider the social network; those who have the informal power; those who have political clout and influence beyond their job title and how you can reach across boundaries to colleagues in other parts of the business.

In identifying these additional relationships, make sure you consider the following types:

- The "go-to" people sought out by other leaders.
- Those who exert influence outside of their title.
- The coaches and mentors for others.
- Those who hold the historical lore about the organization and know how things really get done.

If you are having trouble identifying the informal network, consider the counterpoint to each of these questions—which are the people who are *not* sought out, who are *not* the trusted advisors. This may give you clues as to where the real power resides.

While "modern" social networking refers to online tools, there is an in-house 3D social network that has a huge impact on how business gets done. You must tap into the network with the formal and informal influencers.

Who are leaders within the social network? Well, consider the most recent company event. Who are the people who drove participation by their presence? (When these people chose not to attend, the turnout was poor.) These are the networkers you need to connect with.

Yes, we're being a bit analytical here, but perhaps a better word would be *intentional*. Success is all about intentionality.

Once you've identified who is connected to you, the next step is to identify how your stakeholders are connected to each other. This systematic approach to relationships will have a huge impact when we get to discussing the health of your working relationships, and more importantly, where you might want to focus your time.

Your final relationship map may look more like the following image, where the thickness of the line indicates the strength of the relationship and those in the shaded circles could be considered your critical stakeholders. Without the due diligence of creating this 360-degree relationship map, it can be too easy to focus on those stakeholders who are immediately in front of you and overlook those key influencers in the next department.

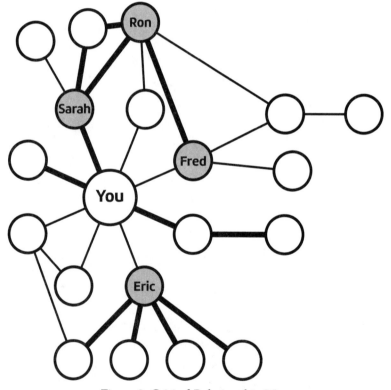

Figure 2: Critical Relationship Map

In this example, the critical stakeholders who may need your care and attention could be Fred and Eric. It may well be that Ron should also be considered a critical stakeholder and therefore a relationship to be developed because of his connection to Sarah and Fred.

The purpose of this is not to list everyone you know but to help identify the right stakeholders, both the obvious and not so obvious! The key is to take the time. Create the map, sleep on it, and show it to a trusted advisor to see if there is anyone you may have missed.

Once you have identified those critical relationships, you are ready to move on to the next step and diagnose the health of those relationships—which relationships are working for you and which are working against you.

Are you starting to see how many people we're dependent on for success?

RELATIONSHIP REVELATIONS

- There are three underlying premises to cultivating winning relationships:
    1. The world of work is a team sport.
    2. You are dependent on others for your success.
    3. Relationships matter.

- We all have critical relationships that can be up, down, or sideways within our organization.
- Peers tend to be the most overlooked relationship—and potentially the most destructive.
- Be intentional and periodically review your working relationships in light of changing priorities and roles.
- Creating a relationship map for each goal or objective will enable you to more clearly see your critical relationships and potential impact for mutual success.

YOUR RELATIONSHIP RESPONSIBILITY: CREATE YOUR RELATIONSHIP MAP

1. Start by listing your key goals and objectives. What are you trying to accomplish? Each goal may result in a different stakeholder map.
2. Next, place yourself at the center of each map. Then start to map each person who may be impacted by (or impact) the achievement of each of your goals. Think broadly and include your manager, direct reports, senior leaders, colleagues, peers from other departments, and matrixed team members. You may start at the group level and then dive down to individual names.
3. Identify the obvious and not so obvious stakeholders:
    a. Consider those who may be two degrees removed from you but connected to your immediate stakeholders.
    b. Who has the greatest impact on your success?
    c. Who influences them?
    d. Who benefits or loses from your success?

Who are your top five stakeholders (not just peers) upon whom you are dependent for your success?

List them below.

1. _____

2. _____

3. _____

4. _____

5. _____

As you consider these people, remember the following:

You are dependent on these people for your success. It is in your best interest to ensure their success.

For more practical resources, go to www.CultivateTheBook.com.

the relationship ecosystem™— the big picture

In a business that is so crazy, to actually know that there is somebody who is really smart, who you care about, who has your interests, and who is rowing in the same direction, is something of immense value. That is an Ally.

« RON HOWARD (ABOUT BRIAN GRAZER) »

The Relationship Ecosystem™ provides a model for understanding the health of your working relationships. In developing the model and our workshop, my goal was to provide a language that enables individuals to discuss how they work together and take appropriate action to improve the quality of those interactions. We're pushing for the following outcomes:

- Ensure agreement regarding the rules of engagement.
- Come to an understanding of what motivates each other.
- Identify the elements that may prevent outstanding performance.
- Increase collaboration, candor, and teamwork in support of clear goals.
- Increase individual resilience and ability to effectively manage change.

The purpose of this model is to place a stake in the ground, a baseline assessment against which assumptions and experiences can be tested, as well as a language to explore what is working and what is not. This model

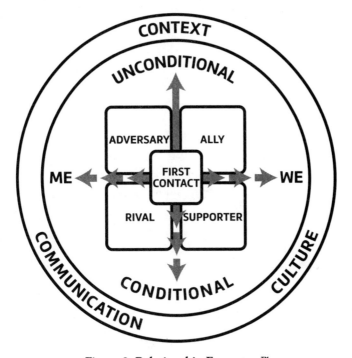

Figure 3: Relationship Ecosystem™

also gives you the ability to assess the level of conflict and tension you are both experiencing, in order to make healthy adjustments.

When it comes to building relationships, the center of the Relationship Ecosystem™ model is the intrapersonal, micro level—the dynamics you may experience with individual stakeholders. The model can be applied to individual relationships and is also applicable with teams.

Before we take a closer look at the center of the model, let's take a step back and consider the big picture. This macro level is shown as the outer ring of the model and focuses on three areas:

- The **context** of your relationships; the history and baggage that comes with preexisting relationships.
- The organizational **culture** in which your relationships occur.
- The **communication** used to describe the relationship; this also refers to the conversation that you will need to have in order to move the relationship forward.

To the more right-brained readers, stick with me. The scrutiny we're giving this topic is designed to expand your worldview, skills, and success! This ecosystem also determines whether a "healthy" or "unhealthy" organization evolves. We can "go with our gut" or try to reverse engineer successful businesses, but if we take time to apply this model to our careers and workplace, we'll grow much faster.

As in any environment, each element of the Relationship Ecosystem™ is interdependent on the other. There is no single, magic potion that will transform the quality of your working relationships! Instead, you will choose from a portfolio of tactics and solutions to drive success.

Peter Senge describes systems thinking as "the discipline for seeing wholes . . . a framework for seeing interrelationships rather than things, seeing patterns of change rather than static 'snapshots.'" Systems thinking is about how everything is connected. When we apply this to relationships, it fundamentally changes the concept of six degrees of separation and results in a new approach that is six degrees of *connection*.

Culture

Your workplace will have both negative and positive aspects. Being conscious of the culture in which you are working is essential to growing a positive environment.

This includes the organizational values, visions, language (jargon and acronyms), systems, symbols, habits, and beliefs (the myths and stories told). These patterns form the basis for how work gets done and what is "normal" in terms of process, behavior, and mindset.

For example, if it's the norm for team members to shout and act disrespectfully toward each other, if gossiping and back-stabbing are to be expected and public dressing downs occur often, then you are likely immersed in an unhealthy culture where destructive conflict is baked in.

In a healthy culture, conflict will still occur, but it will happen in a way that increases understanding. When disagreements occur, they will be handled in a respectful manner that results in strengthened (not damaged) relationships. Candid feedback is the norm, along with a willingness to discuss the undiscussables.

While there are documents that may inform an organization's culture (policies, processes, posters, vision statements, and mission statements), these unwritten rules are usually summed up following a new-hire orientation by a veteran employee who explains "how things really get done around here."

● ● ●

The new operating mindset is six degrees of connection.

● ● ●

They include the elephants in the room or gorillas in the corner—those issues and topics that most can see but choose not to talk about for fear of the repercussions.

An organization's culture affects the way individuals and teams interact with each other, and it has a reach beyond the organization's walls to impact the experiences of customers.

To add further complexity, I often encounter subcultures that may align or conflict with the overarching organizational environment. These subcultures may exist as a result of geographic differences (in an international organization). They are also shaped by individual leadership styles.

Organizations with constructive cultures tend to invest in employees to unlock their full potential, resulting in higher motivation. Employees are confident enough to take informed risks, and mistakes are treated as learning opportunities rather than occasions to punish. Communication is regular, open, and effective. Employees demonstrate a pride in the work they do, the widget they create, and the brand they represent.

The fruits of a healthy ecosystem are easy to spot: innovation and creativity abound, quality is valued over quantity, continuous improvement is the norm, and value and effectiveness are judged at the group level rather than at the individual level.

• • •

In healthy cultures
. . . mistakes
are learning
opportunities . . .
organizations invest
in and develop
employees to unlock
their full potential.

• • •

In organizations with an unhealthy culture there is more emphasis on the tasks to be achieved than the people who achieve them. Success is characterized by individual needs at the expense of the success of the whole group. In a toxic ecosystem, we observe increased stress and conflict within teams. Finding errors becomes a badge of honor. Decision-making becomes more controlling, with decisions made by those with title rather than the necessary expertise. Interactions are about protecting one's turf. Ultimately, performance suffers, for the organization and the individuals working within it.

In the unhealthy organization, asking for help is seen as weakness. Relationships are built around internal competition, tit-for-tat behaviors rather than an aligned team approach. The short-term gains and "me-first" focus always result in the company taking its eyes off the competitive landscape.

Context

Hmaun binegs are craetrues of cnotxet. In fcat, cntxoet is the olny way we are albe to raed. As lnog as the fsrit and lsat lrettes of wrdos are in thier prpoer pleacs, not mcuh else rllaey mttares.

This jumble is an example of how the human brain uses context to process the information it receives, anticipate what will happen next, and determine what actions to take.

Context is why we find it easier to sing along with a song that's playing in the car, rather than singing it unaccompanied. It's why we may remember the name of a business contact when we bump into him or her at work but struggle to put a name to the face at the grocery store on a Saturday afternoon.

Similarly, if we see a certain collection of letters or words, our brains will jump to conclusions about what comes next and try to apply past experience to make sense of what's being seen.

Context is critical when we evaluate our relationships. This history, and potential baggage, will either reinforce an effective relationship or weigh it down.

We expect the other party to respond to our questions, requests, or recommendations just as we respond to theirs. When a relationship is constructive, with a history of positive interactions, this context provides a basis from which the relationship can continue to flourish. In other words, not only does our past experience tell me how you may respond, or what data you will want to receive in any given situation, but also what will cause you to laugh, be engaged, and feel energized.

> • • •
>
> *In unhealthy cultures . . . finding errors and weeding out mistakes becomes a badge of honor.*
>
> • • •

Past context will also tell me what frustrates you, when your energy may lag, and what can be done to turn that around. For example, when a colleague shares her preference for graphs and charts versus detailed data tables, you remember her preferences the next time you are solving a problem together. (I prefer charts and graphs, by the way—in case you hadn't noticed.)

In a baggage-laden relationship, we tend to experience more restrained and guarded interactions. True thoughts and concerns are not shared, the conversation is focused on the facts at hand, and little time is spent on ensuring that those facts are being interpreted correctly. The focus remains at the surface level rather than on uncovering new understanding.

I often work with leaders who have been promoted from within the organization. Yesterday they were peers and friends with other employees; today they are the boss. I have heard many managers say "but we've been friends for years, it doesn't matter." In this situation, however, the nature of the working relationship *does* change.

When you become the boss, the power dynamics shift; at some point you are going to have to give tough feedback to those who were formerly your peers. You will allocate assets from a limited pool of funds and make decisions regarding projects and promotions. Those choices will impact their perception of you and the relationship dynamics.

The move from peer to boss is one of the critical trigger points for a conversation about new rules of engagement; what's staying the same *and* what needs to change. We'll get to some practical tools to prepare for conversations that can preserve your friendship and set it on a new professional course.

Context is developed over time. As we dive deeper in the Relationship Ecosystem™, consider whether the experiences with your current work relationships are "one-off" blips on the landscape or whether they represent a pattern of behavior that you can use to diagnose the health of your relationships.

Be intnetoinal, iedntiyf yuor critiacl satkehloedrs, and ivenst the tmie to get to konw tehm at a dpeeer lveel. Culitvaitng winnnig realitosnhpis hppaens one cnovreastoin at a tmie.

Communication

As we move forward, the words I will use are intended to describe the behaviors you experience in the relationship. They are not meant to be labels or adjectives to be attached to the *person*. We describe the conduct, not the person. Do not box in your coworkers, as this will limit your ability to see opportunities for change.

I have deliberately chosen words that are provocative. The goal is for you to stop and consider the impact *you* are having on others and the extent that this aligns with your intent. It should also cause you to consider how you may be labeling (intentionally or unintentionally) the impact others are having on you.

When relationships are strained, we tend to be less thoughtful in the language we use to describe the other person, both publicly or privately. We tend to portray others as the villains in our stories. Often we choose not to step up to the conversation that would call out inappropriate behavior or adjust the nature of the relationship, allowing the situation to continue to deteriorate. When we do have the conversation, we sometimes rush to speak—potentially causing more damage than good.

I was recently leading an executive development program where one participant shared the challenges she was having with another colleague. The relationship had been damaged through commitments not being kept and by the colleague's explosive reaction when confronted. She was seeking advice on how to improve the relationship, but during her explanation she referred to the other person as "a three-year-old."

With this choice of words, she both labeled the other person as the (immature) villain, and in doing so, disempowered herself from taking positive steps. In perceiving the other person as a child, she was reinforcing her own behavior—and would be perceived as being arrogant. The first step to strengthening this relationship was simple but powerful: changing the language used to describe the other person.

Relationships are built (or destroyed) one conversation at a time.

In my work as an executive coach, participants will often share their struggles with a difficult interaction. When I ask if they have spoken to the other person about their frustrations, the answer is almost always a swift, "No!" or "I tried, but it made the situation worse."

In order to move things forward, we must talk with the other party. If you don't talk it out, you will be acting it out.

Just ask a friend or family member how they know when you are frustrated; I am sure they will have a long list of your "tells." My experience has shown that our "poker face" becomes even less effective in a work setting. Your colleagues know when you are frustrated with them or others. When it comes to relationships, especially working relationships, the old adage "silence is golden" is wrong.

• • •

OWN your relationships . . . Rather than . . . Disown it.

• • •

In developing the Relationship Ecosystem™, my intent was to provide an objective framework that would empower you to pause and *own* your relationships. Later, I will provide you with a tool for framing those conversations. And yes . . . there will be more charts!

Myth Interpretation

I would like to share one final thought before we move on. A failure to understand the big picture can lead us down a destructive path, where others are portrayed as villains and the difficulties we experience are always someone else's fault. This allows us to create the stories that justify our behavior, reinforcing an attitude of "What did you expect?" Attitudes and actions based on these myths will create a self-fulfilling cycle, where a relationship continues to decline with each person hardening his or her opinion.

Remember that the person in the next office may be reading this same book. For them, the difficult relationship they are looking to change may be with *you*.

RELATIONSHIP REVELATIONS

- Cultivating winning relationships requires a pragmatic view, which includes culture, context, and communication.
    - o Culture is the collective behavior of an organization's employees.
    - o Context is the history and baggage in an existing relationship.
    - o Communication is about the language used to describe the relationship dynamics or other party.
- Relationships are built or destroyed one conversation at a time.

YOUR RELATIONSHIP RESPONSIBILITIES

- If you could summarize your organization's culture in three words, what would they be?
- How does your organization's culture support or prevent effective professional relationships?
- Reflecting on past conversations, where did the "baggage" get in the way of clear communication?
- In which relationships are you withholding communication?
- What has prevented you from speaking up?
- What has been the impact of not speaking up?
- Which of your relationships could benefit most from this perspective?
- What is to be gained by both parties if you focus on turning this relationship around?

For more practical resources, go to www.CultivateTheBook.com.

CHAPTER 4

the heart
of the model

*I know enough to know that no man is an island. . . . You
can't be a good leader unless you generally like people. That
is how you bring out the best in them.*

« RICHARD BRANSON »

Let's return to the Relationship Ecosystem™ and consider the heart of the model, to explain the life cycle of relationships from the moment of first contact to where you are today.

First Contact

First contact can be an introduction or initial opportunity to work together. It can also include meeting a stranger (with no prior knowledge), or meeting someone who is "familiar" to you— for example: someone who was been referred to you by another colleague, a transfer to your team from within the company, someone you have met at a networking event, or someone whose reputation precedes them.

When we meet a "stranger," we are neither totally for nor against that person, as our working relationship is yet to be established. We aren't clear about how our goals are aligned.

When meeting someone who is "familiar," we may have heard about that person's reputation (or they about ours) before our meeting. Maybe we've checked out online profiles or asked others in our network about each other. This may influence our behavior and attitude, either causing us to be more restrained or more vocal.

We exchange business cards and make polite small talk; however, in most cases the jury is out. Egos are (somewhat) in check and we are on our best behavior. Conversations will tend to remain at a surface level. Small talk is unlikely to reveal the underlying concerns, hopes, and vulnerabilities of either person. Think of it as "first date" behavior—we try to present our best image.

During First Contact, our relationship may or may not start off on the right track. We may already be biased for or against the other person based on the research we have done, or simply based on our own unconscious biases. (It has been reported that we sum up people within the first few seconds of meeting them, making assumptions about others that ultimately impact our attitude.)

The judgments we make about others, which inform whether or not we wish to move the relationship to a different level, are influenced by a myriad of factors. Whether it be the quality of your handshake, the cut of your wardrobe, or the way you address the waiter, all serve to influence at a conscious and subconscious level.

Whatever the circumstances behind the First Contact, and assuming we move to a "second date," we start to confirm or change our first impressions. The context for our relationship starts to be established, and the behavioral norms are formed. In each and every interaction, the assumptions made during the first meeting are either reinforced or replaced with a new, deeper understanding.

As the relationship progresses, there will come a point when our attitude shifts and the nature of our relationship changes. This may be a readily identifiable moment—the "day we fell in (or out) of love."

The most successful shift from First Contact occurs when there is mutual interest and commitment to do so, when both parties are committed to cultivating a winning relationship. Where the shift occurs through one person's efforts, the results are less effective over the longer term.

Whatever the trigger for change, there are four possible directions the relationship can move—four relationship situations in the workplace that I have either experienced, observed, or had described to me by clients and workshop participants.

THE FOUR RELATIONSHIP DYNAMICS

The Ally: An Ally will have your back at all times and is invested in your success. This is an *unconditional* relationship, one that you can depend on during good and tough times. You are likely to be as invested in your Ally's success as he or she is in yours (although you do not need to be working on the same project).

As a point of clarification, this is not about skipping through the daisies where everything is just wonderful all the time; Allies will give you the tough love as well as the encouragement you need. A true Ally will be the first person in your office to tell you, "Your presentation sucked." They are the ones who hold the mirror to your face and make you take a hard look at what just happened. They then coach you through it and help you fix it. An Ally's motto is "I'm right here with you."

The Supporter: Supporters are fun and nice to work with. They are your fan club, encouraging you and providing feedback—but only when you ask. (Allies will give you feedback whether you ask or not.)

Supporters can be relied upon to help out when times are good. But when the going gets tough, they become more silent and are unlikely to take personal risks to help. You don't want to wait until you are facing a crisis to know whether you have Allies or Supporters around you!

This relationship is **conditional** in nature. A Supporter's motto is "I'm right behind you."

• • •

If you have identified an Adversary or a Rival relationship, don't panic! Keep calm and carry on reading!

• • •

The Rival: The Rival tends to be a little more competitive in nature. In our workshop discussions, participants often identify their peers as Rivals. Rivals behave in a more overtly competitive way, with the competition focused not just on the next promotion but on limited company resources. For example, a Rival may compete with you for budgetary support for a specific project or for the fifteen-minute window of time with the boss.

The competition can manifest itself in many forms. Rivals use verbal or non-verbal behaviors intended to show they are better, stronger, or more qualified than you. Their passive-aggressive approach may lead you to believe you have agreement in a meeting with a Rival, only to discover your Rival has no intention of following through.

This relationship is also **conditional.** When it suits the agenda of the Rival, he or she can work well alongside you. However, when your Rival's agenda is contrary to yours, the working relationship becomes more challenging. The motto of a Rival is "I am ahead of you."

The Adversary: Adversaries are by far the most troublesome and stress-inducing relationships. This is an **unconditional** relationship, in that an Adversary will be challenging no matter what.

Adversaries come in two forms. One is the Overt Adversary, whose actions are right out in the open. You know who this person is. When you know something isn't quite right but may not be able to identify where or who is causing the disruption, you may have a Covert Adversary. In either case, having an Ally looking out for you can be invaluable!

Adversarial behavior can, at the extreme, be malicious, deliberately undermining your reputation. In my own career, a peer was resentful of my promotion to a role he thought he deserved. His adversarial behavior included hiding critical information from me and talking behind my back.

The motto of an Adversary is "I'm against you!"

Frenemies

Personally, I find working with Supporters and Rivals the most emotionally exhausting. The conditional nature of the relationship means that they are inconsistent—the worst of "good cop/bad cop"; you worry about which one is going to show up in the meeting today. When working with a Supporter or Rival, heightened attention to subtle clues can be stressful and exhausting. That is not to say that adversarial relationships are not difficult! But at least you know what to expect and can prepare in advance.

This brings us back to the critical nature of the Ally and the need to intentionally invest in these relationships. An Ally relationship can act as a buffer, support, and stress reliever—protecting us from those relationships that can undermine us.

What if you now realize that you have a Rival or adversarial relationship? Or several? First off, don't panic! In later chapters we'll explore why the relationship may be strained (and what you may be doing to create the situation).

Changeable

Once you move past first contact, all the relationship dynamics intersect and can overlap. Notice there's a solid line between Adversary and Ally and dotted lines between the other types. This is to demonstrate how relationships can move. While it is not impossible, it would take a serious case of neglect for an Ally to turn into an Adversary overnight, and some miracle for the reverse to happen—hence the solid line. Invariably, relationships change over time, usually through a lack of care. It is more likely that an Ally will become a Supporter or Rival before becoming an outright Adversary. In the same way, an Adversary will likely move to being a Rival before becoming an Ally.

While we can't control relationships, we can take what we're learning and be intentional about improving them.

Intent vs. Impact

Action-oriented, with a direct communication style, Ian was having problems in his work relationships. He had the habit of moving rapidly from project to project, and the pace overwhelmed others. He was seen as impatient, dismissive, and condescending—an Adversary at worst, a Rival at best. Unfortunately, it was the Adversary reputation that was proving to be the most sticky . . . Ian was becoming a more frequent focus of hallway conversations.

The Relationship Ecosystem™ was the catalyst for change, along with a candid conversation with both Ian and his boss. We were able to provide insight into his personal leadership style, identify the triggers that resulted in his directive style, and practice strategies to build self-management. As a result, he was better tuned into his own style and aware of others' styles, especially those that differed from his. This helped him slow down and bring others along *with* him, rather than dragging them behind. Ian's reputation started to change, from Adversary to Supporter.

There are very few people whose DNA makes them a natural-born Adversary, someone who gets up in the morning and decides, "Today I'm going to be an against you. I want to be perceived as an Adversary." While this person's intention may simply be, "Time is short; we need to get moving on this project; I need to get the team moving. I need to start giving orders," to the person on the receiving end, this can be misinterpreted as arrogance, directive, and, at worst, adversarial.

Here is another example. When facilitating an Emotional Intelligence workshop, we'll use the example where a colleague continually interrupts someone (a scenario most of us can definitely relate to). I then ask "What's the impact of this behavior? What do you tell yourself about someone who interrupts you?" The answers I hear include the following:

- The person is rude and self-centered.
- The person doesn't care about what I have to say.
- The person is disrespectful and arrogant.

- The person has already made up his or her mind; I may as well stop talking.
- I must be stupid.

When we follow up with, "What is the impact of this situation on your behavior and attitude?" people will describe frustration and withdrawing from the conversation (or from the relationship).

I then ask participants to put themselves in the shoes of the other person and identify whether they think the person's *intent* is to be rude, disrespectful, or arrogant. The answer is often a brief silence followed by, "Well, maybe . . . but probably not."

None of us deliberately seek a reputation characterized as rude, etc. However, some of us end up with this very label. (And yes, I hope you're starting to look in the mirror . . . and squirm a bit.)

The key thing to learn from this example of interrupting others is reinforced every time I use it—for myself. I am a habitual interrupter. After all, I wrote this book so I could just keeeeeep talking, right?

Seriously, I'm getting better at holding in comments while listening to others. In our workshops, people always laugh when I share that the "colleague who interrupts you" is, in fact, ME! While my *intent* is to latch on to the fascinating thing you've just said—and then come back to what you were going to say next—my behavior is likely to result in you shutting down. The relationship is potentially damaged, and I am (mis) perceived as a Rival or Adversary. Certainly not my modus operandi *or* my desire!

Paved with Good Intentions

Here's another example of the difference between the internal point of view, our intent, and the external point of view, our impact. Let's say as part of a leadership program you have been asked to complete a questionnaire to learn more about your preferences. You indicate agreement with each of the following statements:

1. Most rules are simply guidelines.
2. I frequently do things on impulse.
3. People think I'm a non-conformist.
4. I like to be spontaneous.

Your internal dialogue may be something along the lines of "I am a fun, spontaneous individual who enjoys variety and can swiftly change focus to meet whatever new challenges come along."

This is your *intent*. (You see where we're going, don't you?)

However, while some will appreciate this fun-loving, spontaneous approach to life, others will have a different experience. The impact of this approach results in a different label being applied to you, one that might be described as "inattentive to details, resistant to authority, ignores process, doesn't plan ahead, is disorganized, and rarely thinks through the consequences of actions."

• • •

Adversarial relationships don't just happen by chance . . . you are not a victim . . . you have played a part . . . that created the relationship either through action or inaction.

• • •

Intent and impact are powerful when aligned. But when misaligned, both have the ability to undermine your reputation and your ability to develop working relationships. Hence my earlier admonition to avoid labeling the *person*. Rather, consider the dynamics of the interaction when determining the nature of the relationship you are experiencing and, wherever possible, give the benefit of the doubt. Even when faced with adversarial behavior, ask yourself what the underlying intent of the other person might be.

Adversarial relationships don't just happen by chance; if you have an Adversary you are not a victim. You've played a part, either through action or inaction.

When coaching my clients to build stronger relationships, my advice is usually not to go head to head with an Adversary. Instead, I recommend a more prudent approach: influencing the relationship by building stronger relationships with others and allowing a form of positive peer pressure to bring change.

When applying this model to your relationships, give the benefit of the doubt and provide the relationship with a "higher" quality assessment. When considering your relationships, look at the *pattern* of behavior you are experiencing. A single bad experience or tense interaction doesn't mean the person is an Adversary or Rival. A meeting in which a colleague didn't speak up in support of your idea doesn't necessarily indicate a nonsupportive relationship. However, if you recognize a pattern of behavior, you probably have good cause to categorize the relationship as more troubled.

Giving the benefit of the doubt, or assuming positive intent, does not mean you blindly ignore transgressions. Once you are familiar with the Relationship Ecosystem™, you'll be equipped to step in and clarify expectations. There's no need to accuse others of malicious behavior, but you should provide candid feedback to describe the experience. This will ensure that a single event does not become a pattern. More on this later.

The Water Cooler Effect

Let's assume two coworkers are at the proverbial water cooler and are having a less than flattering conversation about a third person (you). It's office gossip about a recent presentation you delivered. Each of the four relationships will respond in a slightly different manner.

The Ally: The Ally will likely step in to stop the conversation, reinforce the company values, and respond with "this is not how we do business around here." They will likely provide a different perspective to counter the negativity. Most critically of all, the Ally will come and let you know what he or she overheard—not to make you feel bad about yourself but in a way that allows you to recognize a potential misunderstanding and take the appropriate action. An Ally has your back, even when you are not around.

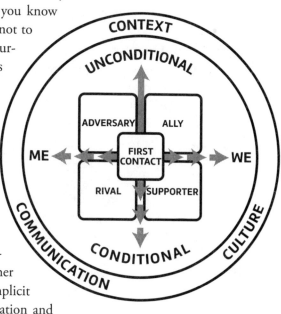

The Supporter: A Supporter will listen to the conversation and may or may not actively participate in the gossip. His or her mere presence provides an implicit agreement with the conversation and the opinions that are being shared. Gossip and speculation hardens into fact. Unlike the Ally, a Supporter *may or may not* let you know there is an issue, and *may not* share what he or she heard. This uncertainty of response can be the most undermining consequence of Supporter relationships. Without the heads-up, you cannot respond appropriately. The rumors continue, and your reputation is diminished.

The Rival: A Rival will be more overt in confirming the worst about what is being said. He or she may even add anecdotes or experiences to the gossip, helping reinforce the "myth" being shared, and in doing so, morph the rumor into fact. They may also share the conversation with others, multiplying the negativity.

The Adversary: If an Adversary didn't initiate the water cooler conversation, he or she will most certainly join in and add fuel to the fire, providing additional examples of mistakes or character flaws. Whereas a Rival may not share with you what was said, you can bet your Adversary will ensure that more people hear about the latest "consensus."

An Adversary may also share the conversation with you, probably in a public setting and with the intent of causing you embarrassment and damaging your reputation. From a career standpoint, it's important to understand that these conversations travel far outside company circles and can impact reputations in an entire industry!

Quality not Quantity

A note of caution at this point—I'm not suggesting your goal is to convert every relationship into an Ally, nor that you be best buddies with everyone and take them home to meet your mother. This is about finding a high road to respectful and effective workplace relationships. If you are not achieving the results you desire, if working with others is not fun, or if candor and debate is destructive, it is essential that you take positive steps.

However, cultivating winning relationships is about quality, not quantity. Many of those we think of as "friends" on our Internet-based social networks are not Allies. Most are acquaintances. According to a study, in 1985 the average American had three people to confide in and share important matters with. By 2006, the number had dropped to two people, with 25 percent of respondents admitting they had no confidante at all.[6]

This point was further demonstrated in a 2012 poll by MacMillan Cancer Support of one thousand people aged eighteen to thirty-five. The poll, published in *The Telegraph*, indicated that while the average Facebook user had 237 friends, only 2 of these could be relied on in a tough situation, with two-thirds of respondents stating he or she had two or fewer really close friends.

One in eight (13 percent) admitted they did not have even a single person who was a good enough friend to rely on if life got very hard. Men (16 percent) were more likely than women (12 percent) to have no one to turn to. About a quarter of people surveyed said they had only one true friend, while one in eight said they had no one at all.[7]

If we put aside the human cost of isolation, the business impact is considerable. Time and cost go up as the quality of relationships goes down, information sharing slows (or stops), silos are created, and decision-making is stalled. It doesn't matter if you're part of a global corporate organization or a local nonprofit—if there is not a culture of trust and collaboration, results are negatively impacted.

Relationships Drive Engagement

Many organizations focus huge blocks of time trying to strengthen employee engagement. One of the earliest proponents of the employee engagement concept was the Gallup Organization. Gallup has studied the indicators of work satisfaction for more than ninety years. The company's latest research included more than 1.4 million employees in 192 organizations, 49 industries and 34 countries. The objective was to identify what effective managers did to create a great place to work. (The four critical dimensions that demonstrated a "successful" organization were employee retention, customer satisfaction, productivity, and profitability.)

The research identified twelve questions used to measure the health of a workplace. Among these, four are integral to the Relationship Ecosystem™:

1. *"My supervisor, or someone at work, seems to care about me as a person."*
2. *"There is someone at work who encourages my development."*
3. *"In the last seven days, I have received recognition or praise for doing good work."*
4. *"I have a best friend at work."*

When the "Gallup 12" survey was introduced, it was this last question that created vocal pushback: "Do I have a best friend at work?" Colleagues readily acknowledged "friends" at work, but the concept of a "best friend" was challenging. This was a business after all; there wasn't time for socializing and creating a "best friend"!

I must admit, I had a similar reaction. I was just transitioning from a fourteen-year career in a finance environment, where the concept of a best friend at work would have been considered bizarre. This was an organization based on data, numbers, and logic; there was no place for emotions or the concept of friendship.

Thankfully, over time, I have come to realize those skills initially dismissed as "soft"—communicating a vision, providing feedback, or leading a team—are fundamental to everything we try to do in business. You don't create a successful, sustainable, and scalable organization unless you can engage the people within the organization to work together.

The "best friend at work" from the Gallup survey correlates with the concept of Ally relationships. In subsequent work, Gallup considered removing the word *best* from the questionnaire, but they found it was no longer a reliable predictor for successful teams.

Gallup[8] also observed that employees who report having a best friend at work were

- 43 percent more likely to report having received praise or recognition for their work in the last seven days;
- 37 percent more likely to report that someone at work encourages their development;
- 35 percent more likely to report coworker commitment to quality;
- 28 percent more likely to report that, in the last six months, someone at work has talked to them about their progress; and
- 27 percent more likely to report that the mission of their company makes them feel their job is important.

You can have the best idea, the most sparkly product, or the most innovative widget, but if you cannot get employees aligned and motivated to produce that product or deliver the service, then your long-term success and sustainability is in jeopardy.

The soft skills are what get the "hard goals" delivered. If you have an Ally, a best friend at work, you are significantly more likely to

- engage your customers;
- get more done in less time;
- have fun on the job;
- have a safer workplace with fewer accidents;
- innovate and share new ideas;
- feel informed and know that your opinions count; and
- have the opportunity to focus on your strengths every day.

And the organizational benefit that comes from all of these BFFs (Best Friends Forever) is well documented. The Gallup research also shows that companies that score in the top half on employee engagement more than double their chance of success. Those reporting engagement at the highest level showed a return almost four times that of the lowest scoring organizations:

- 10 percent higher customer loyalty
- 22 percent higher profitability
- 21 percent higher productivity
- 48 percent lower safety incidents
- 37 percent lower absenteeism
- 41 percent lower quality defects

• • •

Cultivating Winning Relationships isn't just an individual goal; it is a corporate imperative.

• • •

Cultivating Winning Relationships isn't just an individual goal; it is a corporate imperative.

There is plenty of research and data clearly demonstrating that while employees may choose to join an organization because of the brand, benefits, and other perceived rewards, they invariably choose to leave an organization because of their relationship with their immediate supervisor. I would also suggest that people choose to leave when they experience a toxic work environment and when they do not have a strong relationship (an Ally) among their peers.

Employees, especially talented high performers, *always* have a choice of workplace and will experience moments at which they consider whether or not to leave. Whether it's the call from a headhunter, starting their own business, or joining a colleague at another company, these moments of choice happen more regularly than most employers care to acknowledge.

Relationships matter.

RELATIONSHIP REVELATIONS

- There are four relationship dynamics: Ally, Supporter, Rival, and Adversary.
    - o An Ally looks out for you and is invested in your success. It is an unconditional relationship.
    - o A Supporter cheers you on and provides positive feedback when asked. It is a conditional relationship and support may be withdrawn when times are tough.
    - o A Rival competes with you for resources and rewards. Support is conditional, and a Rival may be for or against you depending on his or her personal agenda.
    - o An Adversary can be overt or covert in his or her efforts against you. The relationship is unconditional, and the antagonism is consistent.
- Diagnosing the health of relationships at work, especially with stakeholders, provides the starting point for positive change.
- Cultivating Winning Relationships isn't just an individual goal; it is a corporate imperative.

Your Relationship Responsibilities: Diagnosing the Health of your Critical Relationships

Review your list of five key relationships you made earlier and add people to this list if you wish. Transfer the names to the Relationship Ecosystem™. Use the full grid to show the relative positions of each relationship—i.e., closer to top right for your strongest Ally relationship, closest to bottom left for Rival relationships, etc.

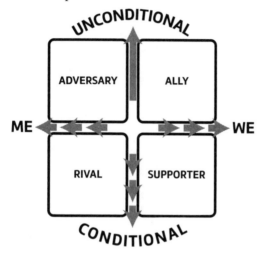

Step 1: Considering your relationships with others

What stands out for you as you look at your Relationship Ecosystem™?
Who is not currently an Ally but needs to be?
If you do not have an Ally relationship, what will your first step be toward developing one?

Step 2: Considering others' relationships with you

Who might describe you as an Ally?
Who might describe you as a Supporter?
Who might describe you as a Rival?
Who might describe you as an Adversary?

For more practical resources, go to www.CultivateTheBook.com.

CHAPTER 5

the ally
mindset

*Every man must decide whether he will walk in the light of
creative altruism or in the darkness of destructive selfishness.*

« MARTIN LUTHER KING »

In his book *Vital Friends*[9] Tom Rath talks about the "Three Friend Threshold." His research found that people with at least three close friends at work were 96 percent more likely to be extremely satisfied with their life. In fact, people would rather have a best friend at work than a 10 percent pay raise!

At the other end of the scale, Robin Dunbar[10], a British anthropologist, found that the average number of effective relationships within communities around the world is about 150 people; this is referred to as Dunbar's Number. In his research, Dunbar suggests that our ancestors found they could more effectively solve problems and defend against predators in smaller groups. Even though humans have the ability to recognize the faces of about 1,500 people, once this 150 person threshold is crossed, the relationships become increasingly casual. They no longer have the deeper connection or commitment that fosters an Ally relationship.

This is not to discount our larger network. I personally make a point of connecting with everyone I meet in a business setting through LinkedIn. At the time of this writing, my connections access a network of more than *10,170,022* professionals. This number is staggering, but these are not Allies. However my 1,500 first-degree connections is a network of established Allies and Supporters (and maybe a couple of Rivals)—individuals who have participated in my programs, colleagues from my time in the corporate world—all of whom would take my call, and I would take theirs.

Through my extended network (the 10 million), I've been able to effect introductions for people seeking expert advice or a new opportunity. I have asked questions and received insight from experts in their fields. As a result of actively cultivating this network, I've made deeper connections with people who are on the way to becoming my Allies and to whom I can be an Ally.

I recently made a new contact, Jennifer, who had moved from Denver (where I live) to Florida. Our paths had not crossed until now. She contacted me as she had stumbled across an old LinkedIn post where I had offered to answer questions and share my story with someone who was considering starting a consulting firm. Jennifer went on to say "I'm intruding by sending an email to see if you might be willing to answer a few questions by email or phone for me. I apologize for taking advantage of a post you made in 2008. . . ." What Jennifer didn't realize was that my approach to life and relationships is one of generosity and abundance (more on these later) and I was more than happy to answer her questions and, as a result, help her move forward more confidently to establish her network and launch her business in a new area where she knew no one: a successful first contact and new relationship.

These "fringe relationships" can be as important as those with people who work alongside me day to day. They offer the opportunity to seek opinions that may be different from those of people who work closely with me. They provide perspective when making decisions or researching new programs.

Ally relationships that start online can be as effective as those that are developed in person. Just think of all the romantic partners who found each other through online dating! I have many colleagues who successfully found their next career opportunity through a LinkedIn status update or a crucial contact who was two degrees of connection away.

• • •

Start by creating and maintaining at least ONE Ally relationship

• • •

What's Your Dunbar Number?

Earlier I asked you to identify your critical stakeholders and the relationships you are dependent upon for your success at work. However large your online network may be, you will likely find that you interact with a relatively small number of people on a week-in-week-out basis. Over time, reaching Dunbar's number of 150 people probably comes quite easily. Remember that this number is an average; there will be those who can effectively manage a much greater number of active relationships. For some of you, though, the thought of managing such a large number of contacts may make your head hurt.

Alone

Following one of my keynote presentations, a participant approached me. He realized, in applying the Relationship Ecosystem™ to his critical stakeholders, that he in fact had *no* Allies, not one. He was both startled at this discovery and somewhat concerned. Until our meeting, he had not given much thought to building *relationships* at work. (This was an engineering firm.) He was very focused on delivering high quality outputs, the *transaction* for which he was hired.

However, as he listened to my talk, he reflected on his career and those of his friends from college. He realized that he had not progressed as quickly as they had and as quickly as he would have liked. Until now, this had not been a conscious thought that required intentional action. Together, we were able to identify a number of tactics he could implement to improve his connection with his five critical stakeholders. As I told this gentleman, my advice is to start with *creating and maintaining* at least one Ally relationship and go from there.

Experience has shown that with the appropriate nurturing, you will end up with more Allies than you thought possible.

Creating Allies

In any interaction, we are sizing each other up and asking ourselves (consciously or subconsciously) four questions. The answers determine whether you, or the request you are making of me, is worth my time, interest, trust, and effort. Essentially, they determine whether or not we will have an Ally relationship. Those four questions are:

1. Can I *count* on you?

    . . . to volunteer, to step up, to be accountable for the
    results you say you will deliver? This is the *reactive*
    perspective. When I ask you to do something will you do
    it (or at least give honest feedback)?

2. Can I *depend* on you?

    . . . to follow through, and deliver on what you have
    promised on time and with the appropriate level of
    quality? This is the *proactive* perspective. If you see a need,
    do you step up and handle it without being asked?

3. Do I *care* about you?

    . . . about your success as much as I care about my
    own. Do I care about about your intent, feelings, and
    emotions? Am I able to empathize, and do we connect at
    a personal level?

4. Do I *trust* you?

    . . . enough to let my guard down and reveal more of
    the real me?

The first two questions are transactional. Do what you say you'll do, and you will meet expectations. The second two questions are emotional at their root and are about interpersonal dynamics. Without a positive answer to the third question and more importantly the fourth, you will struggle to achieve an Ally relationship with that person. Getting to yes with the last two questions is more challenging than simply doing what you said you would do. However, this is what differentiates an acquaintance from a friend, a coworker from a trusted partner, a Supporter—or Rival—from an Ally.

Turn the Table

Consider the critical stakeholder relationships you identified earlier. Can you answer yes to all four questions?

● ● ●

Without trust there is no Ally Relationship.

● ● ●

I am sure that with some people you've immediately sensed *four yeses* after making first contact—it feels like you have known each other for a lifetime. On the other side of the coin, there will be people you'll meet who you don't connect with personally—where "something" warns you to arm your forcefield. Let's call these the *four nos*. There is science behind these emotional reactions. Relationships, by their nature, are emotional at their root. We'll dive into this shortly.

Every interaction is an opportunity to make a deposit to, or withdrawal from, the relationship bank account. Trust is built in the small moments as well as the big actions. Connections grow when we ask and stay tuned-in for the answer, when we invest time in understanding what others do for fun outside of work, when we get to know the person. It is about acknowledging what is happening in peoples' lives *and* delivering what is required at work.

To be an Ally means uncovering what is important to the *other person* and being able to articulate and share what is important to *us*. It is about the conversations you have, as well as the results you achieve.

Who Is an Ally?

Of course, anyone who can help you achieve your goals is a potential Ally. Some are more obvious than others. The following people may already be your Allies:

- People who share a common interest or goal.
- The colleague who is working to achieve the same results.
- The colleague who shares his or her experience and provides coaching.
- The team member who acts as a sounding board for your ideas.
- The vendor or supplier who works collaboratively to help ensure a successful outcome.

But let's be clear: you don't need to be able to help me achieve my goals to be my Ally. I have Allies who have no influence over my success but are there to hear me vent or hold me accountable for taking action. Allies can also be found in unexpected places:

- Someone you meet at an industry event, who readily introduces you to a key contact in his network.
- A colleague who chooses to put aside her immediate priorities to help you complete an important project or achieve a critical deadline.
- The colleague who helps you get time with another leader, and then spends time helping you prepare for success in the meeting.
- The colleague who has moved on to a new company but is still available to provide advice.
- A family member or close friend who listens and supports you through the difficult moments in your life's journey and is there to share the laughter and successes.
- And again, your coffee-Ally, who adds an extra shot of espresso when she senses you need it!

ESSENTIAL QUALITIES: YOUR ALLY MINDSET

We talked earlier about your reputation—the "who knows you?" perspective. Being honest with yourself about how well you demonstrate these qualities is crucial to growing as an Ally and cultivating Allies.

1. *Abundance & Generosity.* This is about working with others, about *being* rather than *doing*. An Ally mindset starts with a perspective of Abundance rather than Scarcity. Do you believe there is plenty of success to go around? Then why not collaborate for the success of others in your company?

This is about moving from a "me first—my success" to a "we first—our success" mindset. Think about it: if we are *both* successful, then there's more success to go around. With an abundance mindset, our hopes and dreams are shared, both personal and business. Our goals and passions are talked about, not kept in the dark, hidden and secret. The more people who know and understand what we are trying to achieve, the more people can help us to get there.

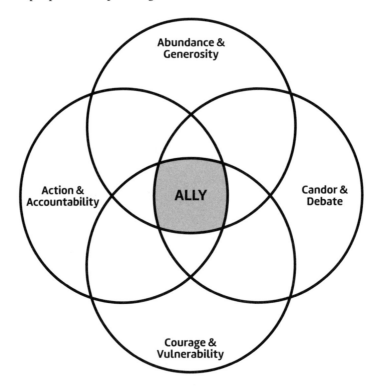

Figure 4: Ally Mindset

Which brings me to Generosity. Abundance alone is not enough. When coupled with generosity, the results can be amazing. Generosity allows us to share our expertise, insight, thoughts, and ideas—our skills—to engage others and help them succeed. Creativity is stimulated as experience, thoughts, and ideas are shared! Continuous learning is an outcome of shared knowledge, increasing the organization's ability to adapt and innovate, and increasing our ability to adapt and innovate. An Ally can be the catalyst for change, which helps transform you and your organization.

Abundance & Generosity are the foundations for my business and my approach to life. Of course, at times I find myself in need of reminders to get back on this foundation. But my Allies are quick to help me shift. I'm often asked who my business competitors are. This is where the abundance mindset comes into play. My answer is that there's plenty of work for all of us. We don't spend time worried about who our competitors are or what they might be doing. I hope they experience success. We have referred our clients to "competitors" who, in my opinion, may be better positioned to meet their needs. This is normal in an abundant world, and it is the right thing to do.

When we approach success as a "scarce resource," it becomes something to be hoarded and not shared. I've seen a "scarcity" mindset undermine collaboration and customer service. How about you?

This leads to the second part of this foundation—Generosity. For me, this manifests itself in the advice, coaching, and encouragement I have provided to those who have asked, even in those in similar businesses to mine. I am happy to share my story, my successes, my failures, my mistakes, my learning—and if this helps you succeed and build your confidence, even better! My focus is on being the best version of me that I can be, to ensure that my team provides the best possible results for our clients. Ask for my input and I will make time for you, because I always learn something from these conversations that helps me to move forward as much as I help you. I am your Ally; I am with you.

Please know that while what I've said above is true, I don't share it to paint myself as Saint Abundance. I've simply seen this mindset do wonders for our business and my Allies!

2. *Courage & Vulnerability.* In an Ally relationship, we need to admit to our shortcomings and mistakes and be open to feedback. This means owning up to our fears or concerns, asking for help, and acting on that help when provided. Vulnerability is not about weakness; in fact, it takes real courage to be vulnerable. Vulnerability comes from the heart—it is a willingness to be our true selves, our best selves.

Waking Up

For me personally, and my Allies, finding the courage to open up was a huge breakthrough. What a relief to no longer pretend to be invincible and all-knowing! Vulnerability is about asking for help when we need it. Vulnerability is about removing the mask with those you trust. Courage is accepting help when it is offered and offering insight to others.

Richard was a young manager who quickly realized that giving tough feedback was even more important than just giving praise. He was in a leadership meeting with one hundred of his coworkers and his new manager. The room was dark, and he noticed his boss at the back, falling asleep. Richard asked around and many of his colleagues commented, "Yes, he has been doing that for years."

He decided to talk to him later that day. At first his manager denied it, but then he acknowledged the embarrassment of falling asleep. A few weeks later, the manager told Richard he'd made an appointment with a doctor and had been diagnosed with sleep apnea.

As Richard reflected on the experience, he was glad he had taken the courageous step to be an Ally to his boss. Other people had noticed and even ridiculed him for dropping off, but they had never brought it to the man's attention, which was holding him back. Constructive, compassionate feedback is important. Being an Ally means having the courage to raise the difficult topics.

Courage & Vulnerability are two sides of the same coin, and they move us beyond a merely transactional relationship.

Banking on It

When I became a bank manager early in my career, I was responsible for a team that lacked confidence. The workers' performance had lagged for some time, and their motivation was low. In my first team meeting, I made the commitment to them that my number one job was to ensure their success.

When I made this commitment, I found that their self-confidence improved almost immediately. The ability to try new things, make mistakes, and learn from those mistakes was increased as a direct result of overt commitment to their success.

Even so, until relatively recently in my career I struggled with vulnerability. Courage was not an issue. If there was a problem to solve or a goal to achieve, I was ready to lead the charge. Courage also manifests itself as being strongly independent and not wishing to be a burden on others. To find my own way forward, I deliberately separated work and home, rarely talking about my family or social life. The idea of admitting to fears, concerns, or weaknesses was unthinkable.

I was afraid that any sign of weakness (remember, I was working in banking, a very male-dominated environment at the time) or vulnerability would result in a mark against me. Instead, I developed an "invincibility cloak." It wasn't until I was coaching a senior leader, who was seeking my guidance on critical decisions impacting both his career and home life, that I was made aware of my need for vulnerability.

He commented on how much he had shared with me, and yet how little he knew of me—as if there was a wall I had put up to protect myself. Busted! He courageously suggested that I learn to open the door, just a bit, and let others in.

Sure, the wall is still there, but it's no longer the fortress of my early career. Do you need to practice courage and vulnerability to have a successful career? The answer depends on how you define success!

3. *Candor & Debate.* This is how we talk about our relationships with others, both what we are saying *to* them and *about* them. It is about having the right conversations at the right time and being able to *hear* the same when it's directed at you. Cultivating Allies is about discussing the undiscussables before they become barriers.

Candor is the ability to share your point of view in a way that increases learning and shared understanding. It requires active listening, a willingness to participate in debate with the intent of helping each other. Candor also means providing and receiving the tough feedback.

It's the difference between "Yeah, your presentation to the executive team was fine" and "Yeah, your presentation to the executive team was fine, but you missed a golden opportunity to talk about xyz when the CEO asked about it . . . you could be much more effective if you did abc."

I thrive on candor and debate—when it is focused on solving business problems. When discussion moves to a more "sensitive" level, about your personal behaviors or work style or how your actions have impacted me on a personal level, I hesitate to speak up. But only for some of my relationships. Why?

In some relationships, it is because I've never sought permission to give direct feedback. This lack of overt agreement about how we work together, coupled with my preference to give the benefit of the doubt and hope things will improve, keeps issues from being discussed.

Recently, we were working for an insurance company where two leaders were having problems. In talking with one of them, we asked, "Have you shared this concern with Fiona?" to which he blurted out, "No! I can't say this to her!" We pointed out the irony that they had worked together for more than ten years and he had known us for only ten minutes. If he could tell us, why not have the conversation with Fiona? They were both stuck in a pattern of behavior and missing out on the benefits of healthy debate.

4. *Action & Accountability.* This refers to following through on the promises you make to others. It's about "doing" behaviors *consistently* with all stakeholders, especially in the difficult interactions, or times of uncertainty. When I ask people to describe an Ally, they can create a list of characteristics quite easily. Think back to the three people you identified as having an impact on you and your career and the characteristics you listed. Easy Peasy, Lemon Squeezy . . . the difficult part is not that we don't *know* what we should do, it's that we don't *follow through* with the required actions. It requires an uncommon discipline to turn that list of characteristics into behaviors that underpin *how* we conduct ourselves.

Being an Ally is not a part-time commitment you schedule for Tuesdays at 2:00 p.m. It is a 24/7 choice. If we continue to pay attention to the first three areas, we will improve the quality of our work relationships . . . a tiny bit. However, to effect sustained change you need to improve in Action & Accountability. Now take a minute and set up coffee with a colleague and ask how you can help them succeed.

Wishes, Ponies, and Unicorns

We all have personal hopes, dreams, and struggles—those things that matter the most to us. It's natural to be guarded for fear of others' reactions. However, in being protective, we lose the ability to engage others in realizing those dreams and overcoming obstacles.

As your Ally, I want to help you achieve your goals, because I know there's an abundance of success to go around. But I need to know about your goals in order to help you.

Within my company, SkyeTeam, we talk about Wishes, Ponies, and Unicorns. It's a phrase that helps us to identify our audacious goals and strive to make them a reality.

As I'm writing this, my team recently started working with our newest, and largest, client. This opportunity came to us through someone who is a graduate of a program I ran a couple of years ago. He saw the "people issues" at the company and immediately called us. He is our Ally. Because of his recommendation for the new client to work with us and his encouragement for us to "think big," we achieved the (unicorn) goal!

Relationship Revelations

- Your Ally mindset is comprised of:
    - Abundance & Generosity: Share your expertise and time to coach others to success.
    - Courage & Vulnerability: Let your guard down to enable learning.
    - Candor & Debate: Discuss the undiscussables before they become barriers.
    - Action & Accountability: Demonstrate the behaviors of an Ally without fail.

Your Relationship Responsibilities

- When it comes to your Ally mindset, what grade would you give yourself in each of these four areas?
    - Abundance & Generosity
    - Courage & Vulnerability
    - Candor & Debate
    - Action & Accountability
- Where are you strongest?
- Where could you pay more attention?
- How often do you censor yourself or withhold feedback for fear of offending others or their potential reaction?
- Where is your comfort zone in being personal at work? What are you OK discussing that extends beyond the transactional, without feeling intrusive or inappropriate?

For more practical resources, go to www.CultivateTheBook.com.

Chapter 6

ally
relationships

*If ever there is tomorrow when we're not together . . . there
is something you must always remember: you are braver
than you believe, stronger than you seem, and smarter
than you think. But the most important thing is,
even if we're apart . . . I'll always be with you.*

« A. A. MILNE, *WINNIE THE POOH* »

What Is An Ally Relationship?

An Ally relationship is unconditional. An Ally is the person who gives you the backing, assistance, advice, information, and protection that you need in order to succeed. They are your support base, the people you can call on in good times, and especially during tough times, and *know* that they will go the extra mile for you.

With Ally relationships, you can survive and thrive in the corporate world; you can get things done faster and more smoothly. Working together with Allies simply helps you, and them, achieve more.

The top ten signs you are an Ally or are in an Ally relationship include the following:

1. The relationship is fun and challenging.
2. When facing a tough situation, she is the first person you call for advice.
3. When celebrating successes, he is one of the first people you call to share your achievements.
4. You are both willing to be open and vulnerable—you understand each other's fears and struggles.
5. You provide each other with the constructive and tough feedback that challenges you to learn and grow.
6. Healthy competition is evident, continually raising the bar to achieve results.
7. The rules of engagement are explicit, and you revisit them regularly.
8. You check in just to see how things are going, without a specific request or need.
9. You are willing to do what it takes to ensure that neither of you fail.
10. You champion her even when she is not present.

On the other side of the coin, signs that you may *not* be in an Ally relationship include:

1. You feel taken advantage of.
2. Trust is being eroded.
3. Debates and interactions leave you feeling bruised and battered rather than inspired and motivated; performance has plateaued.

4. You don't challenge the status quo; you are saying yes when you are thinking no.
5. You don't hold each other accountable; you commit to action but allow those commitments to fall to the wayside.
6. Mistakes result in public admonishment rather than opportunities to learn and grow.
7. You hesitate to provide important feedback for fear of the possible reaction or impact on the relationship.
8. There is no standard for high performance; missed expectations or underperformance are not addressed.
9. You are not able to be your best every day, and your opportunities for advancement are stifled.
10. The other person focuses on his or her agenda and goals; usually at your expense, words and interactions are twisted to suit their purpose.

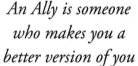

An Ally is someone who makes you a better version of you

The impact of these negative symptoms is that attention is diverted from the value-building activities that drive business performance.

From Me to We

Cultivating a winning relationship starts with the needs of the other person. Be curious about him, what drives him, what his goals are. Explore what is standing in the way of those goals and consider how you may be able to help.

Yes, this means you give before you take or have expectations of value returned. Changing relationships is not about keeping score. Move beyond the transactional or simply focusing on the task of the project at hand. Make the choice to develop a healthy, productive working relationship, to get to know your colleagues as individuals.

CHARACTERISTICS OF AN ALLY RELATIONSHIP

1. Abundance & Generosity: Share your expertise and time to coach others to success.

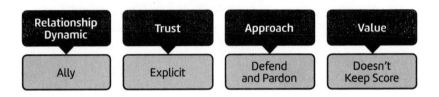

- **Trust: Explicit.** Trust is the underlying premise that drives Ally behavior. As an Ally, trust is given based on commitment—commitment to mutual success.

  Trust is maintained by doing what you say you are going to do when you say it will be done, and doing it to the best of your ability. Trust is knowing that you both have each other's best interests at heart and that this underpins each conversation and action that follows.

  An Ally does not keep score

  While trust may be built and maintained through our actions, it starts by being given rather than earned. Sound backwards? As an Ally, one gives trust from the outset, but this is not blind trust. I may trust my intern to present to my team; I probably will not trust him to present to major clients without additional coaching and support.

- **Approach: Defend and Pardon.** Ally relationships don't always run smoothly; tension, difficult moments, and misunderstandings will occur. Perhaps the feedback provided by your Ally stings and you react defensively. Maybe phone calls aren't returned as promptly as usual or your Ally is less accessible than you would like. The differentiator between an Ally and the other types of relationship is that when these events happen, and when friction and conflict arise, an Ally will give you the benefit of the doubt and assume positive intent.

As humans, we seem to be hardwired to assume the worst when things don't go as planned. An Ally will inquire, check your intent, and avoid making assumptions that may be incorrect. She will defend your honor and forgive mistakes.

- **Value: Doesn't Keep Score.** An Ally relationship is based on mutual, though not necessarily equal, value, in which each party brings something to the party. This value may be in the form of subject matter expertise, personality style, experience, stage of career, or some other factor. This does not mean that the relationship is equally weighted. In an Ally relationship, there is give and take (in that order) *without keeping score.* At times, one person may seem to benefit and receive more value than the other, and this may remain true throughout the whole time the relationship exists. At other times, that balance may switch and change. It doesn't matter—and if it *does* matter to you, then maybe you and your counterpart are not truly Allies. The key to an Ally relationship is that there is more focus on the *collective value achieved* rather than the *individual value received.*

2. Courage & Vulnerability: Let your guard down to enable learning.

- **Authenticity: The Real Me.** Operating from a perspective of authenticity enables you to be your true self and to put aside the mask. In an Ally relationship, you are able to admit the concerns that hold you back, the hopes you are working toward. You admit your mistakes and celebrate your successes. This level of self-awareness and sharing is where vulnerability occurs.

  Being vulnerable doesn't mean that you have to "let it all hang out." What it does mean is that an Ally is someone you know beyond the professional work persona displayed in the office. This doesn't necessarily mean that you socialize outside of work, but you take the time to understand each other beyond the office. You are professional peers who share stories and successes both about work and about home.

- **Success: Throws the Party.** An Ally will celebrate your successes and achievements. He or she is the first to offer congratulations both in public and in private.
- **Ownership: Owns His or Her Part in the Relationship.** An Ally will take the time to sit down and clarify expectations. This conversation is focused on both WHAT needs to be achieved and HOW you will work together to achieve it. There are no assumptions about what is required; the relationship is jointly owned with no finger-pointing and blame if misunderstandings occur. An Ally will be proactive in both initiating and revisiting this critical conversation.

3. Candor & Debate: Discuss the undiscussables before they become barriers.

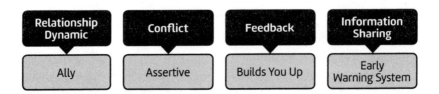

Relationship Dynamic	Conflict	Feedback	Information Sharing
Ally	Assertive	Builds You Up	Early Warning System

- **Conflict: Assertive.** An Ally will take the time to sit down and discuss unmet expectations. A conversation left unsaid only guarantees that the underlying issues will fester and grow. If there are things that frustrate you about how you work together, you can guarantee that the other person has frustrations about you and your working style too.

The moment the implicit rules of engagement are broken and expectations are missed, the relationship is jeopardized. We assume that others know what is expected of them, and so often we are wrong. Taking the time to talk with our colleagues, *especially* those with whom we have had a long-term relationship, is important. New projects and new goals may require new ways of working together. Instead of turning it into a guessing game, it is in your best interests to be explicit up front.

True Allies will revisit the rules of engagement on a regular basis, recalibrating based on current and future needs.

Feedback: Builds You Up. An Ally is a truth-sayer, willing to provide you with feedback on an immediate basis, celebrating your successes as well as your misses. He or she will help you explore decisions you need to make and ensure you consider all perspectives. An Ally will address a conflict situation with you head-on, before it becomes an issue that damages the relationship (with your Ally or with others).

The role of an Ally is not just to be your advocate. It's easy to be an Ally in the good times, when things are going well. A true Ally is someone who can provide "tough love" too. If there is feedback you *need* to hear (but maybe don't *want* to hear) an Ally will find a time, place, and way to provide you with that feedback. And then he won't leave you hanging—he will explore your options, help you to navigate the situation, and coach you to new action.

• • •

An Ally will give you the feedback you NEED to hear

• • •

One of my clients described this as the difference between being nice and being kind.

Being *nice* is the realm of the Supporter; tough messages are either not shared or diluted to such an extent that the feedback is no longer useful. Being *kind* means that I share the message, even if it may sting, because not doing so would leave you in a far worse position.

An Ally will

- trust that the intent of the feedback is to be constructive;
- trust that the feedback will be seriously considered; and
- model authenticity and vulnerability.

Shares Information: Early Warning System. An Ally will ensure relevant information is freely shared and endeavor to prevent the predictable surprises, by providing a heads-up. An Ally will coach you on how to present to a critical audience. When you vent about an issue, an Ally will help you stop and think it through and ensure that you take the necessary steps to correct the situation.

4. Action & Accountability: Demonstrate the behaviors of an Ally without fail.

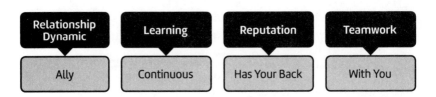

- **Learning: Challenges You to Raise Your Game.** An Ally will challenge you to stretch your performance. He or she will explore creative solutions that enable you to overcome obstacles. Whether that is through encouraging you to apply for a new role or a promotion, or accept increasingly complex projects, or simply challenging you to spend additional time preparing for an important presentation, she is helping you be your best. She helps you discover who you can become!
- **Reputation: Has Your Back.** As you saw with the water cooler example, a true Ally will have your back—even if you are not in the room. An Ally will present your point of view, or an alternative explanation, to those who may have an issue with your perspective. He is also the one who will let you know where concerns about your reputation are occurring.
- **Teamwork: With You.** An Ally is consistent; you can call on her and *know* she will step up to help. An Ally can help you out directly, for example, by stepping in to provide an extra pair of hands to complete a project, or indirectly, by placing a call to introduce you to someone in her network. At other times an Ally will understand that action isn't required and will simply listen.

For You

When I ask people in my programs, "What is the benefit of having, or being, an Ally?" The understanding is clear. Self-confidence is increased. In a culture of mutual success, people report feeling empowered to take action. They no longer look over their shoulders, worried about what others are saying or thinking—because they *know*.

"My Ally helped me through a difficult project at work; she mentored me. Without her I would not have been successful."

"My Ally let me see the possibilities in a new role."

"I was struggling with my customer presentations and how to overcome objections. My Ally took the time to role-play with me. Without him I wouldn't have stayed in sales."

"I wouldn't be in this career today but for the candid feedback from my Ally. She made me see how others (mis)perceived my approach and what was being said behind my back. I hadn't realized there was a risk of burning bridges with people in my network. I am forever thankful that she had the courage to hold up the mirror and help me take a hard look at myself."

"My Ally knew I was interested in moving into a finance role and introduced me to a number of her contacts who had open positions on their finance teams. Without my Ally, I would not be in my current role."

As we move through our careers, especially as we become more senior within organizations, the need for Ally relationships becomes more critical. As we move up through the organization, the pressures become bigger, the complexity of the decisions we make increases, and the ripple effect of our leadership brand impacts more people across the organization and beyond. At the same time, the candor and feedback we receive can decrease. Without a cadre of Ally relationships, risk increases—not just personal risk, but also risk for the team and organization.

There are also demonstrable health benefits to having an Ally at work. When compared to employees who don't believe that coworkers will help them during times of stress, those who have best friends at work identify significantly higher levels of healthy stress management, even though they may experience the same levels of stress (Rath, *Vital Friends*).

If you believe you're in an Ally relationship, one of the most powerful things you can do is find a way to tell the other person that you are his Ally, and what he can expect from you as such. Telling someone that you have his back makes the implicit explicit. It empowers; it removes assumptions. It results in enhanced confidence and an even stronger relationship.

A word of caution: saying "I am your Ally" (or whatever words work for you) can be like saying "I love you," so make sure you mean it. If your words and actions don't align, you can damage the relationship. Trust may be reduced. Also, we all know what is expected next when we say "I love you"—the other person is supposed to say "ditto" (as in the movie *Ghost*). Be prepared for the possibility that this may not happen immediately. Instead there may be awkward silence or, "Oh, OK, thanks." You have read this book; your colleague may not have. Explain the context around your declaration. Let her process it. I promise your relationship will be stronger as a result.

I recently had the opportunity to hear Dr. Brené Brown speak on the concept of vulnerability. She shared a personal story of a friend who called and told her, "You are a friend who would move a body for me." Essentially, her friend was saying, "You are my Ally; I am your Ally." Making that declaration, being explicit about the nature of their friendship, was a defining moment for that particular relationship.

For the Organization
An Ally relationship is based on mutual respect. Both parties learn from, and contribute to, the relationship. In my experience, Ally relationships at work can and do extend into friendships outside of work; however, this is not always the case or a requirement.

An Ally is someone with whom you enjoy sharing ideas, knowledge, and experiences. He or she is central to you achieving your goals. An Ally is the person whose opinion you respect and value. Whether or not he is an expert in your field, he brings a perspective that broadens your horizons.

As a result, in teams and organizations where Ally relationships abound, creativity and innovation increase when the fear of looking foolish is reduced. Candor and debate increase, ensuring that shared learning is increased. A learning organization is a growing organization, one that is nimble and able to anticipate changing market situations.

In a team or organization that encourages Ally relationships, people are on the same page and pulling in the same direction to achieve results.

That's not to say that competition no longer exists. It does. In those teams and organizations where an Ally mindset is encouraged, competition actually increases. However, it is a healthy competition—one that builds capability and delivers exceptional results. Employee engagement is high, and people actually look forward to coming to work.

Collaboration and teamwork become the norm. Organizations that leverage the language of the Relationship Ecosystem™ experience a reduction in silos, turf wars, and organizational politics, which slow down information flow and decision-making. Conversations that question the status quo are encouraged and not hidden behind closed doors.

《 》

What could be achieved in your organization if everyone was focused on the organization's goals, on pulling together rather than looking over their shoulders, worried about who was about to undermine them?

Relationship Revelations
- Ally relationships go beyond the transactional; they are personal.
- Ally relationships are focused on the "collective value achieved" rather than the "individual value received."
- Organizations that cultivate Ally relationships grow in their competitive capabilities.
- Cultivate at least one Ally relationship.

Your Relationship Responsibilities
- Reflect on your insights from this chapter. What does an Ally relationship look like to you?

Your Ally Relationships
- Review your list of critical stakeholders. Who is not currently an Ally but needs to be? What will you do to cultivate a winning relationship with this person?
- Given your deeper understanding of the characteristics of Ally relationships, what names would you remove or add to your list?
- If you do not have an Ally relationship, what will your first step be toward developing one?

You As an Ally to others
- To whom are you an Ally? How would that person know that you are his or her Ally?

For more practical resources, go to www.CultivateTheBook.com.

CHAPTER 7

supporter relationships

It is the first law of friendship that it be cultivated; the second law is to be indulgent when the first law has been neglected.

« VOLTAIRE »

Definitely Maybe

A Supporter relationship is conditional . . . sometimes (like my sense of humor, I suppose). When times are good and risk is low, you can rely on your Supporters. When the going gets tough, you discover that some Allies are actually Supporters. One day your Supporter is "right there with you," working shoulder to shoulder, and the next, they are "right behind you."

The top seven signs you may be in a Supporter relationship include:

1. Fun without challenge.
2. No news or only good news—feedback is limited.
3. The relationship remains mainly transactional.
4. You say (or hear) yes when you should say (or hear) no.
5. Uncertainty as to whether the person will respond or step up when you need it.
6. You hesitate before providing tough feedback.
7. The status quo prevails and average performance becomes the norm.

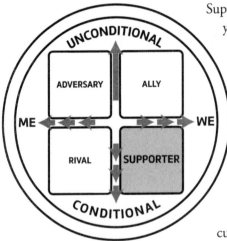

Being a Supporter is the easiest relationship dynamic to adopt and demonstrate. Likeability can be the goal of a Supporter—saying "please" and "thank you" and completing tasks as required. Moving a Supporter to an Ally comes as the result of a deliberate choice—by them and by you—to move beyond the transactional.

All's (Not) Well in the Health Care World

We worked with the leadership of a health care company, who described their organizational culture as "family-centric." The long tenure of most employees, and a Supporter approach to relationships, had resulted in complacency. Feedback, especially the tough feedback, was not part of their culture. Individuals and teams worked around the less effective employees rather than holding them accountable, or providing coaching.

The impact of this was a steady decline in market share, initially blamed on external economic conditions. While there was no doubt the recent recession was having an impact, it was the lack of candor in the organization that masked systematic failings with processes, products, and people.

A conversation with the senior team to explore the concepts of the Relationship Ecosystem™ brought about a sense of urgency to change the culture of the organization and more closely align with its corporate values of truth and transparency. Providing leaders and managers with the appropriate coaching support, training, and tools to create a culture of candor resulted in an improvement in business results, employee engagement, and accountability.

Characteristics of a Supporter Relationship
Understanding is critical in diagnosing your relationships and applying the appropriate prescription for healthy change.
1. **Abundance & Generosity: Share your expertise and time to coach others to success.**

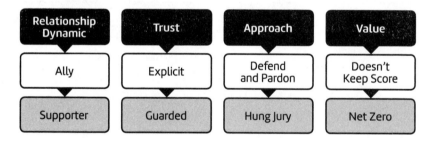

Relationship Dynamic	Trust	Approach	Value
Ally	Explicit	Defend and Pardon	Doesn't Keep Score
Supporter	Guarded	Hung Jury	Net Zero

- **Trust: Guarded.** A Supporter is your cheerleader; she will provide encouragement for you, your ideas, and your successes. A Supporter will likely keep your confidences when asked to do so. Like an Ally, a Supporter is usually fun to be around. However, there is a point at which the limit of trust is reached. This may not be easy to articulate, but my coaching clients describe a "something" that's missing from the relationship that prevents true closeness and honesty. There is a hesitation before sharing personal stories or exposing vulnerabilities. Trust is guarded.

- **Approach: Hung Jury.** When things don't go according to plan, a Supporter may not jump to negative conclusions, but he is unlikely to assume positive intent. While he may not contribute to gossip, he may not rush to your defense either.

- **Value: Net Zero.** With a Supporter relationship, the net value gained is zero, a neutral outcome in which neither party really gains. This can be attributed to the lack of challenge, candid feedback, or drive to improve performance.

2. Courage & Vulnerability: Let your guard down to enable learning.

- **Authenticity: A Mask.** Conflicts may occur, but they are the exception rather than the norm. Supporters will tend to maintain harmony and avoid tension, but this appearance may be misleading. They will be unlikely to share their personal challenges or concerns. If you ask a Supporter, "How are you?" you will likely hear "fine" in response. The mask of positivity is maintained.

- **Success: Joins the Party.** A Supporter is not necessarily going to lead the celebrations or promote your achievements to others. She is more likely to pause and assess how others are responding before joining in.

- **Ownership: Owns Their Part in the Relationship (if Asked).** A Supporter tends to be focused on maintaining the status quo and is likely more reactive than proactive. This means if you initiate a conversation about the relationship dynamics, the

Supporter may initially push back and deny that anything needs to change. With encouragement, he may participate, and you may reach a new understanding toward an Ally relationship. However, do not expect a Supporter to initiate this conversation. Remember, the very concept of cultivating positive workplace relationships is new territory for most people, including you!

3. Candor & Debate: Discuss the undiscussables before they become barriers.

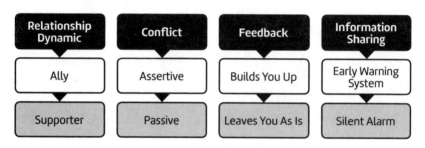

Relationship Dynamic	Conflict	Feedback	Information Sharing
Ally	Assertive	Builds You Up	Early Warning System
Supporter	Passive	Leaves You As Is	Silent Alarm

- **Conflict: Passive.** Unfortunately, Supporters will avoid taking personal risk when things get difficult. This "safety first" mindset can undermine others.
- **Feedback: Leaves You As Is.** A Supporter may avoid raising the difficult issues for fear of conflict. This is the difference between being nice and being kind. Being nice is the realm of the Supporter; tough messages are not shared, or else they are diluted to the point that the feedback is no longer useful.

  • • •

  A supporter will leave you in the same place you arrived.

  • • •

  Being kind, the realm of a true Ally, means the message is shared even though it may hurt (because it could make you stronger and more successful). A Supporter usually leaves you in exactly the same place as you arrived.
- **Information Sharing: Silent Alarm.** Whereas an Ally will provide you with warnings of impending disaster, a Supporter tends to sound a silent alarm, perhaps assuming you already have

the information you need. She might drop subtle hints but will be unlikely to step in with a "Don't do that!" or "What were you thinking?"

4. Action & Accountability: Demonstrate the behaviors of an Ally without fail.

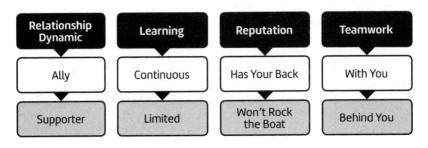

- **Learning: Limited.** Without the candor of an Ally relationship, the status quo prevails. There is little healthy competition. As a result, *average* becomes the new norm, and innovation and creativity suffer. A Supporter can be a great listener, but the backing stops there. Because of this, a Supporter may (unintentionally) create a victim mindset in you.
- **Reputation: Won't Rock the Boat.** As discussed earlier, a Supporter is unlikely to speak up in your defense if you are not present. This may not always be an issue. However, when others may be questioning your capabilities, this can lead to an impression of agreement. This tacit acknowledgment is influenced heavily by the seniority of your Supporter. Paying attention to your relationships up, down, and across the organization is important in order to avoid this situation.
- **Teamwork: Behind You.** When the going gets tough, when the situation becomes complex, where personal risk is involved, a Supporter may step back from you. When your reputation is being tarnished, he may not have the courage to speak up. When there are warnings of potential disaster you need to hear about, he will fail to share them in a timely fashion.

The Impact of Supporter Relationships

In my opinion, the Supporter relationship is the most insidious relationship dynamic.

Really, Morag?

Yes. A Supporter relationship tends to be comfortable and easy, and this comfort may result in complacency and a misplaced sense of security. It may not be until the moment of need when your Supporter realizes, "Whoa—I didn't sign up for this . . ."

When a Supporter isn't there for us, we tend to be shocked, because it's unexpected. However, the fault is ours for not cultivating conversations and assessing the health of the relationship. While I have characterized Supporter relationships as insidious, this is only the case when we make incorrect assumptions. Remember, most Allies begin as Supporters.

For You

In low-involvement relationships (those that don't directly impact your immediate goals or priorities), having Supporter relationships may not be an immediate issue. In fact, we all want a broad number of Supporter relationships. Let's consider them Allies-in-waiting.

When those Supporters are in our high-involvement stakeholder group, the impact can be far-reaching. Over time, we may find that Supporter relationships actually undermine trust. We stop reaching out and asking for input because the response doesn't challenge us.

There is a risk that we will become complacent and start to believe the positive feedback we hear from our Supporters. When we don't receive balanced feedback, our weaknesses and blind spots go unacknowledged, our performance suffers, and our careers stall.

For the Organization

When working with my clients, I find the organizational culture to be a good indicator of the health of working relationships within that company.

Where Supporter relationships are the accepted norm, our client organizations often find themselves stuck. Average performance becomes acceptable, innovation stalls, and the organization loses its competitive edge. When we don't step up to the tough conversations and provide the feedback that others need to hear, how can we hope they will step up their game?

While information may be shared, it occurs at a superficial level. Because of this, the quality of decisions tends to suffer. Mistakes are seen as one-time events. What is missed is the connection between these events. Little time and attention is spent in seeking to understand the underlying causes. The fire may be put out, but there is surprise when it reignites.

My client organizations that recognize the Supporter mindset across their business describe their culture as "like a family." But as we dig in, we see that this can be a justification to avoid tough conversations. I am not discounting the value of a family culture, one that generates a sense of belonging. However, even the best families are not harmonious units all the time. Healthy families have moments of tension and arguments that address the important issues.

An organization that focuses solely on (false) harmony misses the opportunity to grow. Trust is built when appropriate action is taken!

Relationship Revelations

- Supporters are a conditional relationship; when the going is good they are with you; when the going gets tough they are behind you.
- A Supporter relationship is insidious when there is not a clear understanding of the health of the relationship.
- A network that consists mainly of Supporters may result in complacency and average performance because of a lack of candor and challenge.
- An organization that is Supporter-based experiences false harmony, which results in status quo and achievement of short-term results at the expense of long-term success.

Your Relationship Responsibilities

- Reflect on your insights from this chapter. What does a Supporter relationship look like to you?
- What is personally at risk for you in having a network that comprises Supporters?
- When has the action of a supporter caught you unawares or surprised you? What needs to happen to ensure that you are not blindsided in the future?

Your Supporters:

- Identify two colleagues with whom you have a Supporter relationship.
- What is it that these colleagues do, or don't do, that leads you to believe they are Supporters?
- What would it take to move them closer to being an Ally?

You as a Supporter:

- To whom are you a Supporter?
- What circumstances cause you to choose to be a Supporter rather than an Ally to that person?
- What would it take for you to become that person's Ally?

For more practical resources, go to www.CultivateTheBook.com.

Chapter 8

rival
relationships

Whenever you're in conflict with someone, there is one
factor that can make the difference between damaging your
relationship and deepening it. That factor is attitude.

« WILLIAM JAMES
AMERICAN PHILOSOPHER AND PSYCHOLOGIST, 1842–1910 »

What Is a Rival?

A Rival is a relationship with elements of adversarial behavior or conflict, but not on a consistent basis. It can be confusing to be on the receiving end of a Rival relationship, which may appear positive one moment and full of tension the next.

This is a demonstration of the conditional nature of Rival relationships. There's always a reason why people act the way they do, but it can be difficult to reflect on what has caused the change, and the reason may not be apparent. This is why having an Ally is critical since your Ally may be able to provide a healthy perspective.

All of us adopt competitive behaviors at different times in our working lives. This competition can be healthy, designed to raise our game. There will be times when you have a different point of view from a colleague. Sharing that different perspective and participating in the debate that follows does not make you a Rival. Rival behavior tends to be destructive; it seeks to position one person over another when it benefits the Rival.

Honest debate with an Ally can still be a heated, in-your-face interaction, but the outcome is increased understanding. At the end of the conversation, the relationship is intact and can even be strengthened. With Rival relationships, when differing opinions are discussed, the focus and debate moves to win-lose. Relationships are tarnished, and one party, at least, will leave the debate feeling bruised.

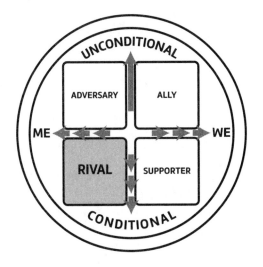

Rival behavior becomes a problem when:

- Differing points of view are aired in a way that stifles debate or causes others to hesitate before speaking up (sarcasm or passive-aggressive behavior, for example).
- Arguments are focused on who is right and who is wrong, and the parties involved are unable to take a step back to identify where they can agree (even if it's agreeing to disagree).
- Disagreement becomes the norm; i.e., we arrive at the meeting ready to fight, rather than focused on the business decision to be made.
- One party leaves the debate feeling "less than" about themselves.

Rivals differ from Adversary relationships in a number of ways. Generally speaking, Rivals do not tend to act with malicious intent toward the other party. They are simply out for themselves and their own personal goals, and if others get trampled in the process, this is perceived as an unfortunate side effect.

The rivalry may be about such things as securing an increased budget, ensuring resources such as headcount are allocated to the Rival's team, or simply getting the rare five minutes of face time with the boss. Your Rival's rationalization of this me-first approach will be "this is business." Experience has also shown it's easy for a Rival relationship to deteriorate and become adversarial.

On occasion, Rivals may not be aware of their negative impact. I've seen these people shocked and mortified when receiving feedback about their behavior. Because it wasn't their intent, they were willing, and even eager, to discuss a new way forward. Remember, someone with a me-first attitude is not necessarily out to get you; they're simply not thinking about you.

Pay attention to your gut reaction while offering the benefit of the doubt to the other person. And consider these signs that you may be in a Rival relationship:

1. They only reach out to you when they need something from you—their focus is transactional.
2. You experience stress and anxiety as you prepare for meetings with the individual.

3. You find yourself gossiping to others about interactions with this person.
4. You approach interactions defensively with your guard up, ready for a fight.
5. You hesitate to share information or provide feedback for fear of their reaction.
6. You do not care whether they succeed or fail.

Case Study: Rival Team Members

David had recently completed the graduate intern program for a major mining organization and was moved into an operational role to manage a team of engineers. This new role was his first management position and required him to lead a team of ten people, including employees who had been with the company for decades.

One member of his team, Stephen, had applied for the manager role and thought it should have gone to him rather than the "fresh out of the box" intern. Stephen and his friends on the team ensured that David's first few weeks in the role were uncomfortable. Their behavior was subtle—creating rumblings at the back of meetings and fostering a lack of urgency to carry out David's instructions.

When things didn't improve at the end of the first month, David decided he had to take action. The team's performance was declining and his manager was asking questions. David chose the courageous route. He decided to have a direct conversation with Stephen and clear the air. He found an opportunity to meet Stephen offsite, on neutral ground. He started the conversation by expressing his concerns and desire that they discuss their working relationship. He listened as Stephen shared his frustrations at being passed over for promotion, and he empathized with him. David then pointed out that it was the company that had put them both in this situation, not either of them.

David offered to coach Stephen to help him overcome the perceived gaps in his style. David then stated that he needed a commitment from Stephen to move from the Rival approach he'd been exhibiting to one that was more supportive. After some thought, Stephen agreed. When David was advanced to a new role nine months later, Stephen was promoted to lead the team.

Characteristics of a Rival Relationship

1. **Abundance & Generosity: Share your expertise and time to coach others to success.**

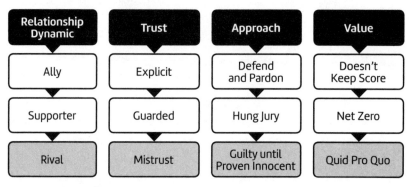

Relationship Dynamic	Trust	Approach	Value
Ally	Explicit	Defend and Pardon	Doesn't Keep Score
Supporter	Guarded	Hung Jury	Net Zero
Rival	Mistrust	Guilty until Proven Innocent	Quid Pro Quo

- **Trust: Mistrust.** A Rival relationship is conditional. If the circumstances suit your Rival's personal agenda, he or she will work with and for you (unlike Adversaries, who will be against you no matter what). Fluctuation in the relationship dynamics results in mistrust.

- **Approach: Guilty until Proven Innocent.** As you will recall from the earlier water cooler examples, a Rival may not necessarily *start* the gossip. However she may add fuel to the fire. How she chooses to assess your interactions will likely focus on where you have fallen short of expectations. This evidence is collected, and it is likely to be shared at a time that will undermine your credibility. Your Rival's approach can be described as "I told you so," as she calls into question your capabilities and deflects issues from herself or her team.

- **Value: Quid Pro Quo.** Rivals keep score, like a CPA-wolf hybrid. They count favors they provide and are expecting some in return. Each interaction is evaluated in terms of the potential benefit or payback opportunity. This is in direct contrast with an Ally, whose focus is on *your* value first and subsequently on the mutual win.

2. Courage & Vulnerability: Let your guard down to enable learning.

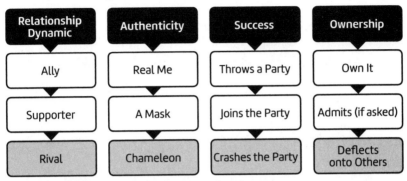

Relationship Dynamic	Authenticity	Success	Ownership
Ally	Real Me	Throws a Party	Own It
Supporter	A Mask	Joins the Party	Admits (if asked)
Rival	Chameleon	Crashes the Party	Deflects onto Others

- **Authenticity: Chameleon.** Rivals are adept at navigating the political landscape in a way that elevates their reputation with decision makers. Rivals may demonstrate chameleon-like behaviors, promising one thing in person and then delivering (or not) to a different standard or timeline. These tactics may be designed to undermine your success, but they can also be a result of focus on your Rival's goals at the expense of others. Don't take it personally, but know how to recognize Rival behavior.
- **Success: Crashes the Party.** A Rival likes to be associated with success. You can expect Rivals to provide back-handed compliments. I recall an all-employee meeting where one executive was giving recognition to members of the broader team (those who did not report directly to him). An award was handed over, to applause from the audience, with the executive remarking, "Of course, you only achieved this because of me. I could have done so much better."

  It may have been a nervous attempt at humor during a high-profile event, but the damage was done. In one breath, the compliment was given and then immediately undermined. This is Rival behavior in action—attempting to steal the limelight.
- **Ownership: Deflects onto Others.** If success is an opportunity to steal the limelight, there are also times when Rivals will seek to deflect attention away from themselves. Rivals will tend to blame others rather than take personal accountability for missed results or poor relationship quality. They will usually have an

arsenal of excuses to demonstrate how the other party let them down. This may be one of the most undermining behaviors. While a Rival may sit down and discuss the rules of engagement and how you are going to work together, he will not necessarily maintain those commitments or revisit those conversations. When friction occurs (and it will) a Rival will likely choose not to air his concerns until an initiative has trouble. When this happens, he will share his frustrations, usually in front of others.

3. Candor & Debate: Discuss the undiscussables before they become barriers.

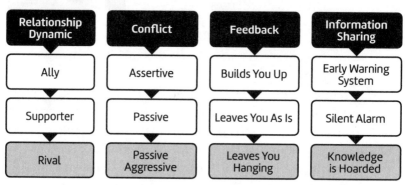

Relationship Dynamic	Conflict	Feedback	Information Sharing
Ally	Assertive	Builds You Up	Early Warning System
Supporter	Passive	Leaves You As Is	Silent Alarm
Rival	Passive Aggressive	Leaves You Hanging	Knowledge is Hoarded

- **Conflict: Passive Aggressive.** A Rival can enjoy the role of devil's advocate when it comes to your ideas. At best, this provides you with perspective, and warnings of impending disaster that you may not otherwise have identified. At worst, it becomes *critical,* undermining confidence and slowing down decision-making. Also be alert for an unusual lack of candor, since your Rival may be opting to watch you fail.
- **Feedback: Leaves You Hanging.** A Rival may provide perspective when asked directly, but the feedback may only be part of what you need to hear. Her approach may not be dishonest, but errors of omission may occur.
- **Information Sharing: Knowledge Is Hoarded.** A Rival works on the basis that knowledge is power. As a result, information is shared sparingly. Ideas are withheld and only shared when there is personal gain or a direct request. This "need to know" behavior can manifest in many ways:

o Not providing resources (people, budget, etc.) in support
of an initiative.
o Sidelining individuals and teams, or closely controlling
decisions within their field of expertise.
This behavior is designed to exclude rather than include
others in the process.

4. **Action & Accountability: Demonstrate the behaviors of an Ally
without fail.**

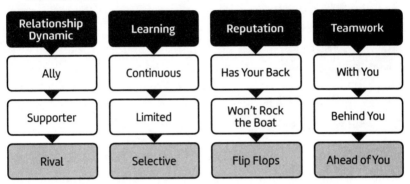

Relationship Dynamic	Learning	Reputation	Teamwork
Ally	Continuous	Has Your Back	With You
Supporter	Limited	Won't Rock the Boat	Behind You
Rival	Selective	Flip Flops	Ahead of You

- **Learning: Selective.** A Rival tends to overlook the importance of continuous improvement. She is likely to believe she is successful *because of* her style and *in spite of* your contribution. She is likely to dismiss the need to collaborate, attend programs, or read the latest book or article.
- **Reputation: Flip Flops.** A Rival may take part in the water cooler conversations regarding you. Sometimes he may start these conversations or add anecdotes of his own. A Rival may pass on the rumors he hears without checking the facts.
- **Teamwork: Ahead of You.** During each interaction, a Rival is focused on what's in it for her. When it comes to teamwork, while she may give the appearance of a collaborative approach, in the final push, it will be about taking the lead and finishing ahead of others.

The Impact of Rival Relationships

A reminder: the term *Rival* describes the behaviors, *not* the person. If we label an individual, this will undermine our ability to objectively cultivate change. We may have portrayed the person as the villain in our own story. This leaves us with two options when managing the relationship—to play the role of the martyr or the victim. Neither of these two roles serves us well.

The victim mindset prevents us from taking action. It keeps us from speaking our truth and having a conversation to reset expectations. The martyr mindset is used to justify poor behavior or a retaliatory approach. The "I had no choice; he backed me into a corner" excuse loses sight of the impact our response has on others. The greatest positive impact a Rival relationship can provide is to raise our curiosity, to induce us to ask ourselves, "What can I learn from this relationship?"

We cannot control others, but we do have control over ourselves and how we choose to respond to a person. When you reflect on your Rival relationships, consider which role you're playing in response—the Rival, the victim, or the martyr? The biggest challenge is for us to stay true to our Ally mindset and behaviors; not to respond in kind, or to give up, but to step up to the conversation that brings positive change.

For You

In our coaching, I ask clients to imagine they're about to go into a meeting with a Rival and share what they are feeling in that moment. Some of the answers I hear include:

"I am feeling defensive in planning my strategy for the meeting."

"Stress and anxiety—will this person make me look foolish again?"

"I am working out how to put him in his place and how I can win."

"I am thinking about the competition, but I now realize it isn't healthy competition."

"I am feeling angry—at her, at me, and at the whole situation."

Take a moment to consider your own experiences with a Rival. How does working with a Rival impact your attitude? How does it impact your focus?

When we're focused on our Rival, when tactics are about winning, we are not focused on the business decision at hand. Innovation suffers as we become more internally focused on this individual, rather than on the big picture.

A Rival relationship tends to be competitive by nature, but there can be positive benefits! A Rival may cause you to move out of your comfort zone and push you to be better. However, unlike the healthy competition in an Ally relationship, only one party tends to grow.

For the Oganization

I have worked in many organizations, across industries and oceans, both as an employee and as a consultant. In each company there was in-fighting, organizational politics, silos, turf wars, and unhealthy competition. All of this slowed down the organizations' performance and diminished the results of everyone involved.

You can have the best product or service, but if you cannot get your people *pulling together*, performance will suffer and the success of your business will be jeopardized. When doubt, mistrust, organizational politics, or toxic behaviors are not addressed, relationships will fall into the spiral of dysfunction. Rival or Adversary behavior will spread.

In my research, the businesses that were able to successfully navigate economic storms were the ones where relationships were already strong, where Rival behaviors were rooted out, and where internal competition was healthy and encouraged excellence.

The ability to cultivate winning relationships will maintain personal engagement and contribute to ongoing success for your entire organization.

Relationship Revelations
- Rival relationships are conditional.
- Competitive behavior alone does not indicate a Rival relationship; destructive conflict does.
- Rival relationships will tend to fluctuate between Supporter and Adversarial behaviors; including political maneuvering, gossip, information hoarding, and turf wars.
- The destructive competition inherent in rivalries often impairs individual and team performance through a preoccupation with winning or saving face.

Your Relationship Responsibilities
- How has having a Rival relationship inspired or motivated you to raise your game and performance?

Your Rivals: Identify two people at work with whom you experience Rival behavior and would like to cultivate a more effective relationship.
- What will happen to your job effectiveness and satisfaction if those relationships *do not* improve?
- If you haven't attempted to address concerns, why not? What is holding you back?
- What characteristics of the Rival relationship are of greatest concern to me? What has the greatest impact on my ability to be successful?
- What would it take to move this relationship toward Supporter or Ally status?

You as a Rival:
- In what situations, and to whom, do you behave as a Rival?
- Describe a situation where you demonstrated Rival behavior. What caused you to behave this way? What was the impact?
- What would it take for you to become that person's Supporter or Ally?

For more practical resources, go to www.CultivateTheBook.com.

CHAPTER 9

adversary relationships

It pays to know the enemy—not least because at some time you may have the opportunity to turn him into a friend.

« MARGARET THATCHER
BRITISH PRIME MINISTER (1979 – 1990) »

How does an Adversary differ from a Rival? In most cases an Adversary will act with *deliberate intent*. His or her attitude is consistently unsupportive.

This behavior may be overt—you, and others, know it's happening and who the Adversary is. Or it can be covert—you know something is wrong, but you cannot identify the perpetrator.

We all end up with an Adversary at some point during our careers; hopefully you will not experience more than one. You know you are in an Adversarial relationship when:

1. You are always looking over your shoulder, wondering when the next hit is coming.
2. You are continuously presented with roadblocks that make it difficult for you to succeed.
3. Your recommendations are met with opposition at every turn, and for no apparent reason.
4. Your Adversary openly criticizes you to others and revels in your mistakes as evidence of your incompetence.
5. You experience hostile behavior and highly charged interactions.
6. You find yourself avoiding the individual.
7. You are focused only on his or her needs and concerns in meetings.
8. Conversations are more like a one-way monologue, with little acknowledgment of your point of view.

A relationship rarely starts this way. I admit there are a few people on this planet who seem to revel in the reputation of Adversary. However, in the vast majority of cases, an Adversary relationship occurs as the result of action or inaction on your part. Yes, I said *your part*. There is often culpable negligence, which can include a failure to

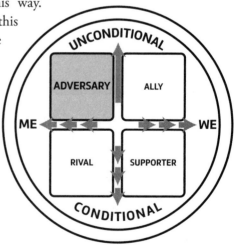

- identify the deteriorating health of the relationship;

- take a look in the mirror to honestly assess what role you've been playing;
- recognize the urgency needed to clarify expectations; and
- take the appropriate action to course correct before the relationship becomes dysfunctional.

Adversary relationships don't just occur across the organizational chart. I've heard stories of Adversaries who started out as Allies and then "turned" against their colleagues (yes, leaders have asked me for advice on how to handle an Adversary on their own teams).

Who are your potential Adversaries? Which relationships do you worry about? Who do you gripe about after work? Which professional relationships are preventing your work life from running smoothly?

In this chapter, we'll be unveiling the langauge and toolkit necessary to take action in Adversary relationships. We can mitigate the impact of these relationships and even transform them into Rival, Supporter, or perhaps, Ally relationships.

CHARACTERISTICS OF AN ADVERSARY RELATIONSHIP

1. **Abundance & Generosity: Share your expertise and time to coach others to success.**

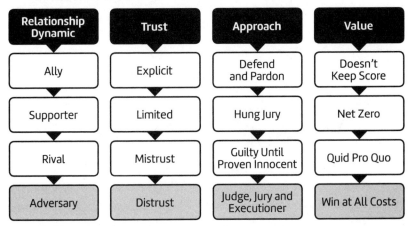

Relationship Dynamic	Trust	Approach	Value
Ally	Explicit	Defend and Pardon	Doesn't Keep Score
Supporter	Limited	Hung Jury	Net Zero
Rival	Mistrust	Guilty Until Proven Innocent	Quid Pro Quo
Adversary	Distrust	Judge, Jury and Executioner	Win at All Costs

- **Trust: Distrust.** An Adversary's behavior erodes trust and may ultimately destroy it. Adversaries do not trust others and will likely portray problems as being the fault of the other party.

- **Approach: Judge, Jury, and Executioner.** Mistakes and failures made by others are treated with contempt and used to undermine others' reputations. Adversaries may recognize that their own behavior is contrary to expectations, but they are able to justify it as a result of others' failings.
- **Value: Win at All Costs.** In an Ally relationship, the score is irrelevant. In an Adversarial relationship it's all about taking and only giving where you *have to*. The focus is on the individual value received rather than the collective value that could be created.

2. **Courage & Vulnerability: Let your guard down to enable learning.**

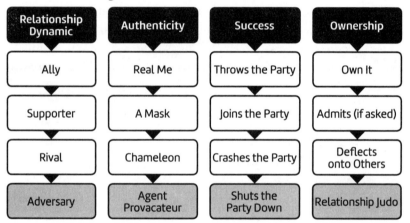

Relationship Dynamic	Authenticity	Success	Ownership
Ally	Real Me	Throws the Party	Own It
Supporter	A Mask	Joins the Party	Admits (if asked)
Rival	Chameleon	Crashes the Party	Deflects onto Others
Adversary	Agent Provocateur	Shuts the Party Down	Relationship Judo

- **Authenticity: Agent Provocateur.** In some ways, a true Adversary can be described as authentic—what you see is what you get. There is no pretense of wanting to work well with you. An Adversary may openly provoke conflict in order to achieve a result.
- **Success: Shuts the Party Down.** If the Rival is about taking the limelight, the Adversary is about taking the limelight, microphone, and curtain call. I recall one company celebration where the Adversary sat at the side of the room, deriding the achievements of those being honored. It was a horrifying display that no one addressed in the moment. Instead, the event came to an early conclusion, with everyone feeling awkward. The vast

majority of those attending knew the atmosphere created was
terribly unhealthy, but they lacked the framework and tools to
address the behavior.

- **Ownership: Relationship Judo.** An Adversary relationship
operates at a purely transactional level. The transaction, when
it needs to occur, is unlikely to go smoothly. If you need something from an Adversary, obtaining it may feel like pulling
teeth from a donkey. If they need something from you, expect
demands rather than requests, with short timelines. An adversary is unlikely to share their personal stories, experiences, or
thoughts with you. There is a clear demarcation that takes these
off the table.

3. **Candor & Debate: Discuss the undiscussables before they
become barriers.**

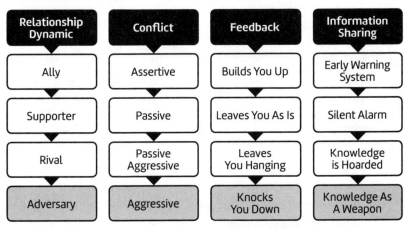

Relationship Dynamic	Conflict	Feedback	Information Sharing
Ally	Assertive	Builds You Up	Early Warning System
Supporter	Passive	Leaves You As Is	Silent Alarm
Rival	Passive Aggressive	Leaves You Hanging	Knowledge is Hoarded
Adversary	Aggressive	Knocks You Down	Knowledge As A Weapon

- **Conflict: Aggressive.** An Adversary will invariably start a debate
on the offensive, with a direct attack against the issue or person.
Conflict may also be allowed to fester, potentially infecting
others with a biased perspective.
- **Feedback: Knocks You Down.** Adversaries are unlikely to
provide constructive feedback. When feedback is provided, it
will be predominantly negative, and the delivery will be blunt.
When feedback is given to an Adversary concerning his or

her own behavior, the individual will likely become defensive, claiming it's someone else's fault.

- **Information Sharing: Knowledge as a Weapon.** An Adversary, like a Rival, works on the basis that knowledge is power. However, an Adversary will take this one step further—knowledge is used as a weapon. Information is shared (or withheld) so that it can have the greatest impact in undermining the success or reputation of another.

4. **Action & Accountability: Demonstrate the behaviors of an Ally without fail.**

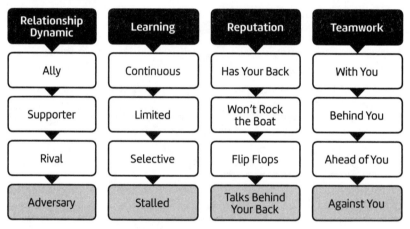

Relationship Dynamic	Learning	Reputation	Teamwork
Ally	Continuous	Has Your Back	With You
Supporter	Limited	Won't Rock the Boat	Behind You
Rival	Selective	Flip Flops	Ahead of You
Adversary	Stalled	Talks Behind Your Back	Against You

- **Learning: Stalled.** There are times when an Adversary is a high performer, able to produce results in spite of the damage to relationships. The Adversary will use these successes as an excuse to maintain his or her approach, claiming that others need to "toughen up." This defensive approach can make it difficult to take the necessary action toward an Adversary, but it needs to happen. Short-term results cannot be allowed to hold the organization's long-term success hostage.
- **Reputation: Talks behind your back.** An Adversary will not hold back in sharing their perception of you and will openly criticize you to others.
- **Teamwork: Against You.** Adversaries tend to focus on their agenda rather than that of the team.

Drained

Having an Adversary will sap your energy for work. It's both mentally and physically exhausting to be on heightened alert to sabotage. There is science behind the emotions that are evoked, and while we can't prevent them, we can learn to mitigate them.

We could use the analogy of firefighting and the risk from individuals who actually demonstrate arsonist tendencies—creating a crisis they can then solve. If we extend the firefighting correlation to an Adversary, I'll advise you not to fight fire with fire. The long-term consequences to your reputation will outweigh any short-term benefit you may experience. Remain professional, however justified you may feel about a retaliatory strike.

Instead, take the time to consider the dynamics of the relationship and your role in the situation in order to identify actions you can take.

For You

I have seen competent leaders doubt themselves when faced with an Adversarial relationship. They started focusing on avoiding mistakes (that could be used as evidence against them) rather than taking informed risk. What a tragedy that these leaders blamed themselves for having an Adversary (they believed that if they were smart enough, they wouldn't experience one). IQ has no bearing on whether or not you'll experience an Adversarial relationship, and a victim mindset only keeps us from changing our game.

Even if you are fortunate enough not to be the direct target of an Adversarial relationship, allowing these behaviors to continue will ultimately impact your reputation as a leader. As others watch the drama unfold, they will be asking themselves, or others, "Why don't they do something about it?" In this scenario, *you* are "they."

For the Organization

Gallup research estimates that "actively disengaged employees" cost the US economy nearly $382 billion each year. Adversary behavior, whether individual or collective, always results in a degradation of standards and a toxic work environment, which will cause your high performing employees to leave.

- The gaps between individuals and teams widen, potentially splitting the organization.
- Information flow slows down as the battle lines between individuals are drawn.
- Decision quality deteriorates and results are delayed.
- Business issues lose focus, and people issues carry the spotlight.
- Confidence in leadership is diminished.

When relationships go sour, everyone suffers. Adversary relationships do not remain private, and at some point others will have to choose a side. This collateral damage not only erodes morale and performance; it can damage the company's reputation when former employees share their war stories with the world!

Relationship Revelations

- Adversarial relationships rarely start out as such; they generally result from action or inaction on your part.
- Characteristics of Adversary relationships include withholding support, empire building, provoked conflict, blaming, a lack of candor, and personal attacks.
- The reputations of those *not* involved in an Adversary relationship can still be tarnished by not addressing the behavior.
- Adversary relationships are not just a personal issue; they are an organizational issue.

Your Relationship Responsibilities

- What collateral damage have you observed as a result of others' adversarial relationships?
- To what extent is your work impacted by adversarial behavior?

Your Adversaries: Identify one or two people with whom you experience Adversary behavior and would like to develop a more effective relationship.

- Describe your last interaction with an Adversary. How did you respond? What was the impact on your relationship?
- If you were to give the benefit of the doubt, what would be the other person's intent?

You as an Adversary:

- Describe a situation when you used Adversarial behavior. What caused you to behave that way? What impact did your behavior have on others?
- What is the impact of Adversarial behavior for you?

For more practical resources, go to www.CultivateTheBook.com.

Chapter 10

emotional, intelligent, or both?

Anyone can become angry—that is easy. But to be angry with the right person, to the right degree, at the right time, for the right purpose, and in the right way—that is not easy.

« ARISTOTLE »

I will admit, I was a real skeptic when I first read Daniel Goleman's book, *Emotional Intelligence: Why It Can Matter More Than IQ.* As compelling as the book was, I assumed it was just the latest fad. I was wrong on many fronts.

Emotional intelligence (EQ) is not, and was not, a new concept. The term may have been new, but the research on multiple intelligences in addition to IQ has been ongoing for decades.

Speaking of emotions, it frustrates me when others describe these foundational competencies as "soft skills" or say things like "that touchy feely stuff . . . when do we get to the group hug?"

There is nothing soft and fluffy about the level of a person's emotional intelligence. It is not about being "nicer," less emotional, or even unemotional. It is about intentionally using the awareness of emotions to enhance job satisfaction and performance.

Unless you run on electricity, emotions are part of your day. You've known someone who was considered a high potential contributor (talented and bright) but who did something to sabotage his or her success. Have you ever been in a conversation that started to heat up fast? Later that evening, you may have thought, "Why didn't I do this?" or "Why didn't I say that?" You might have wondered, "If *I'm* so smart, how do these things happen?"

> • • •
> *We can all be smart after the event; emotional intelligence is about being smart* in the moment.
> • • •

When confronted with a stressful situation, the brain has the inherent tendency to react out of habit (only more intensely). We keep talking when we know we should listen. We move to action when we know we should stop and consider the options. We say yes even when we know we should say no.

We can all be smart *after* the event; however, emotional intelligence is about being smart *in the moment,* especially in the face of uncertainty and challenge.

When careers stall, a lack of technical skills is rarely the sole cause. People fail when they don't achieve results, especially during seasons of conflict and tension.

Who Goes There: Ally or Adversary?

Imagine you are walking down the street. Around the corner comes your archenemy, your Adversary.

- What are you thinking and feeling in that moment?
- What happens to your behavior?

When I ask this during my workshops or as part of a seminar, I hear the following responses:

What I am thinking and feeling:	What I do (my behavior):
"I immediately think about how I can avoid them." *"I can feel the hackles go up on the back of my neck; I am remembering our last (stressful) interaction."* *"Depending on what's happened, I start to feel angry or frustrated."* *"I dread having to talk to them."*	*"I cross the street!"* *"I pretend to be on the phone so I don't have to talk to them."* *"I avoid eye contact and hope they didn't see me."* *"I walk quicker—so I get past them sooner."* *"I can feel myself start to frown."* *"If I have to talk to them, my answers are short and curt."*

Now, let's imagine it's your best friend, your Ally, who turns that corner.

- What are you thinking and feeling in this scenario?
- What happens to your behavior?

In this situation I usually hear the following types of responses:

What I think and feel (my emotions):	What I do (my behavior):
"I'm excited to see them; I immediately think of some news I want to share." "I'm pleased to see them." "I start to smile." "I am remembering our last (productive) interaction." "I feel happy!"	"I make eye contact." "I smile and wave so that they know I have seen them." "I walk quicker—so I can get to them sooner." "I'm open and eager for the conversation and to catch up on news since we last spoke."

Even in a workshop setting, each time I ask the second question, many people in the room immediately start to smile. Just the thought of seeing their friend triggers an immediate emotional response, which then triggers a behavioral response (which reinforces the emotional response, and so on).

Contagious

Your emotions don't just impact how you feel about yourself. Your emotions also affect the interactions you have with others. Think about it: when you are feeling down, you probably have someone you can call, the "happy-go-lucky" person who gives you a pep talk that always leaves you with a smile. There may also be people in your office who have the ability to drain the life force from those around them.

The Latin root of emotion is *movēre* which means "to move." Let's face it, feelings drive behavior, performance, and our ability to cultivate winning relationships. If you don't take this into consideration in your quest for effective work relationships, you can inadvertently sabotage your own efforts or become frustrated.

I use the diagram on the next page to show the overlapping relationship between emotions, our behavior, the results we achieve, and the impact we have on others (our reputation).

Sure, we can squelch emotions for a time, but eventually the energy will leak into behaviors. Verbal examples may include the raising of your voice or how your voice shakes when you are nervous. Even if you choose not to talk it out, through your body language you are still signaling to the world just how you feel! (Whether it be rolling your eyes when your Rival or Adversary starts to speak or changing body posture and letting out a sigh of frustration.)

This is especially relevant when you're anticipating a difficult interaction, experiencing conflict, or attempting to function in the midst of uncertainty. Rather than reacting impulsively, emotional intelligence will enable you to plan your approach and will greatly improve the chance of a successful outcome.

Self-awareness and self-management are about emotional self-control: regulating reactions and impulses. Even with an understanding of emotional intelligence, you will have good days and bad days, but with practice there will be fewer Jekyll and Hyde moments.

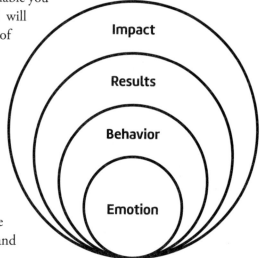

From Me to We

When I am working with individuals who are experiencing difficult relationships or unhealthy competition between teams, I often hear, "They need to go first" or "If they weren't so difficult to deal with I could . . ." Cultivating winning relationships is about taking responsibility for your actions, your personal leadership, and your need to learn from others.

If you have ever found yourself saying, "I wish I had known he felt that way" or "I was only joking!" then this is a sign that your social awareness needs improvement. By the time you've had this thought, it's too late—the situation has escalated and you now have a damaged relationship to repair.

When there is a lack of empathy, when we don't work to understand the needs of others, we lose trust. If I don't know what you're thinking and feeling, I trust you less. I may create real or imagined barriers between us and, as a result, more distance. This is when silos form, and Rival and Adversary behaviors become more apparent. It seems that we are predisposed to remember the negative emotions and memories far longer than the positive ones. This was useful when it was a matter of life or death, not so much when we are in an office environment.

We recently worked with a team that lived up to all that Rival and Adversary relationships can provide: broken promises, back chat, ignoring emails. Some team members even had large files that contained every note and transgression others had made toward them. They were all trapped in this cycle of negative emotions. It was highly charged and highly toxic. What surprised us all (including the team) was just how quickly the transformation to Supporter relationships was. A matter of weeks and committed efforts by the team members to have the candid conversations needed to let go of past baggage and look forward to the possibilities meant that conversations and relationships became less strained. It is still a work in progress, but the team, to their credit, is working more effectively. It is a solid Supporter environment, and one that is commited to moving closer to Ally if at all possible.

When you demonstrate empathy and respond to the needs and feelings of other people, you *gain* their trust, build collaboration, increase candor, and enhance results. These are the fruits of an Ally culture.

The Science

There is science behind our emotions. Understanding this is vital to mastering our emotions and our personal success. It starts with an appreciation for the basic physiology of the brain. The human brain has three main parts:

Part 1: The Brain Stem

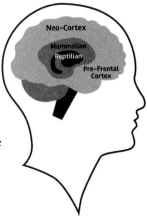

The first part of the brain is the brain stem, which sits at the base of the skull. It's the most primitive part of the brain and is responsible for basic functions such as temperature control, breathing, heart rate, balance, and reflexes. It is referred to as the reptilian brain. It doesn't think; rather, it acts out of instinct (which is a good thing when we are asleep) and focuses on keeping us alive. It is what allows a goldfish to swim around and around the fish tank going, "Oh, a castle . . . oh, a castle . . . oh, a castle."

Part 2: The Limbic System

Sitting above the brain stem is your amygdala (Greek for "almond," because it is almond-shaped). It's part of the limbic system, the emotional center of the brain. It is the mammalian brain and the site of emotional memory and emotional learning. This area of the brain houses your short-term memory and both controls and expresses emotion. It answers one critical question of human survival, "Do I eat it or does it eat me?"

This is better known as the fight-or-flight response. It determines your actions in situations in which you feel threatened and selects your response to danger; it also determines your potential response to good news and positive stimuli. I like to describe the limbic system as your dog brain, which helps explain why your retriever is pleased to see you when you get home from work while your goldfish is still saying, "Oh, a castle!"

Emotional learning is based on past experience and helps you decide what things to embrace and what to avoid, creating a library of experiences and reactions from which the amygdala can pull. As we age, this emotional learning library increases in size. However, it tends to be a library stocked with past reactions rather than offering new approaches to situations. This is partly due to the fact that while the limbic system has the ability to remember dangers and your responses to them, it is not "smart," in that it is not capable of complex thought. Instead, it's like a computer program—"if A, then B." The limbic system will repeat past reactions unless you find a way to break the program, to unlearn and relearn new ways to respond.

Part 3: The Neocortex

The third part of the brain is the neocortex, particularly the prefrontal cortex. This part of the brain is most evolved in human beings and is what differentiates us from all other animals. The neocortex enables you to develop and demonstrate collaborative social behaviors, to innovate and create the tools to thrive in different environments, to adapt our surroundings to meet our needs, and to support our success.

This is your rational brain, where your intelligence resides; it is the site of your working memory. It is where you do your higher-order thinking. Our language centers are located here, and the neocortex is what enables you to plan ahead, solve problems, and have visionary ideas.

The Amygdala Hijack

All information coming into the brain first passes through the amygdala and limbic system—every experience, every sensation, every observation. The amygdala acts as your threat-detection radar. This filter is *always* on, operating subconsciously to protect you from dangers, both expected and unexpected.

If no threat is detected, then the information goes to the neocortex for processing. The billions of connections within the limbic brain and the thinking brain allow for the free-flow of information and for you to manage complex thoughts.

When the brain detects a potential threat, it prepares the body to either fight that threat or run away from it. Each of us has a tendency toward one default behavior or another, based on our earliest childhood experiences, our upbringing, and our past experiences, whether personal or observed. We then determine what will best protect us in that moment.

● ● ●

Emotions are a crucial guide to important decisions. Logic alone is not enough.

● ● ●

If you've ever walked into a room and just *known* that something was wrong, without necessarily being able to articulate what the reason was, then you were experiencing your limbic system and amygdala at work. There is science at work here that explains the gut reaction. The vagus nerve connects the brain through your neck and chest to your stomach and is the trigger for the knot in the stomach (or butterflies), the tightening in your chest, or the constriction of your throat. These physical symptoms are designed to warn you about a perceived threat.

When the amygdala is triggered, the nervous system causes numerous bodily changes, such as an increase in blood volume, rise in blood pressure, increase in blood glucose, and blood clotting agents (as well as the release of hormones, including cortisol and adrenaline). Blood is redirected away from your brain and internal organs and is sent to your limbs in preparation to flee or fight.

Less blood to the neocortex actually inhibits your ability to think clearly. Looking back on a volatile situation, you might say, "I had no choice." It is also why you only think of the smart reply—what you should have said or done—some time later, when these chemicals have started to dissipate (from twenty minutes to a few hours, depending on the level of intensity).

Emotions are a crucial guide to important decisions. Logic alone is not enough. It is the amygdala that determines whether we should react to the information based on past experiences stored in our emotional memory or send it to the thinking part of our brain, the higher-leveled neocortex, for further processing.

Frequent Flyers

Here's an example of emotional memory: Let's go back to evolutionary times. You're a Neanderthal and you are walking with your Neanderthal friend on a gathering expedition. You hear a rustle in the bushes. Suddenly a saber-toothed tiger jumps out and eats your friend. What do you do? You run to the nearest tree, of course! It's your flight response.

The next day, you're walking through the field again and hear a rustle in the bushes. What do you do? Regardless of what actually caused the noise this time, you run to the tree. Your brain formed a neuropathway and an emotional memory: rustle in the bushes equals danger, which means run to the tree.

There aren't any saber-toothed tigers in the workplace today; however, your limbic system doesn't know they are extinct. When faced with a real or perceived threat, your emotions override your thoughts. Think about your relationships at work, as far as your limbic system is concerned. A Rival or an Adversary can easily be perceived as the modern-day equivalent of a saber-toothed tiger.

While the threats that a Rival or Adversary present may not be life-threatening, your limbic system nonetheless perceives them to be real. The threat could be aggressive words and interactions, body language, or social—the risk that they will make you look bad. If you perceive you were slighted in a previous meeting, if your interactions have been tense and conflict has become the norm, your emotional memory resurfaces each time you meet with, or even think about, that individual.

A Hijack in Action

During a debriefing exercise during a workshop, a throwaway comment by one participant, Simon, implied that another participant, Fiona, talked too much in meetings. Fiona promptly started to cry and left the training room—an immediate and powerful amygdala hijack that triggered a flight response.

To say "you could cut the air with a knife" was an understatement. The other participants looked at each other, also hijacked (as was I!). It was a real life moment from which we could all learn. I let the tension sit for a moment and then asked the class, "How do you want to handle this? What do you need to do next, to soothe your amygdalae and repair any potential damage to the relationship with Fiona?"

I'll give this group credit—they stepped up to the moment. Simon immediately went to find Fiona and apologized (as did the group when they both returned to class). They discussed what had just happened and how it made them feel—shocked at the immediate negative impact, powerless to know how to restore the camaraderie and fun atmosphere they'd been enjoying. They also faced the sudden realization that any of them could have made a similar throwaway comment with similar devastating results. They were *all* responsible for taking action to restore the relationship, not just Simon, who had made the initial comment.

When Fiona returned, she had the courage to share her experience and what had triggered her powerful reaction (threat equals flight), which had surprised her too! Fiona had recently received feedback that she had a tendency to speak first and dominate conversations. As a result of that feedback, she had been focusing on listening more and talking less, so the comment had really hit home. She did not feel valued and felt that she was failing—context the group didn't have, but once shared, provided perspective.

The class concluded successfully, and I followed up with everyone about a week later. While not wishing this incident on anyone (including a facilitator), the demonstration could not have been better. Being able to coach the group through the situation ensured that relationships were maintained and ultimately strengthened.

What Triggers You?

Those hot buttons that trigger your amygdala may not be rational to others, but in the moment they are very real for you, and the resulting amygdala hijack can be debilitating.

We recently went to watch a play at a local theatre. When I walked into the auditorium, I was immediately hijacked: our seats were very high up, and what was worse, the architectural design of the auditorium included grades that only exaggerated the open air, up in the air feeling. Our seats felt more like a "shelf with a view" than a "room with a view."

● ● ●

Many triggers are situational; if you can master your emotions in one, then you can learn to master them in the stressful environment.

● ● ●

My vertigo was immediately triggered, and while the rational part of my brain knew that the building wasn't going to collapse, my amygdala fired and determined that my life was in imminent danger. It took a lot of concentration and coaxing from my family to get to my seat, and more time for me to regain control of my heart rate and the sick feeling in the pit of my stomach.

Eventually I did regain control, and the show was fantastic. I had a similar reaction on my first trip through Terminal 5 at Heathrow Airport. The new terminal has walls, and floors . . . of glass! Definitely not designed with vertigo sufferers in mind. I can now walk through the terminal easily, but the first few trips had me asking other passengers to escort me across the floating bridges while I closed my eyes. I'm not kidding.

At work, our triggers are no less impactful. The most frequent ones shared during our programs include:

- Perceived slights and disrespect from other colleagues. For example, being interrupted or left off a meeting invite.
- Your project is cancelled after weeks of hard work.
- A customer (or colleague) snaps at you unfairly.
- Your best friend (and coworker) is laid off suddenly.
- Your boss assigns you more work when you're already overloaded.

Consider your personal hot buttons. How many are situational, meaning they only occur at work, but not at home, or vice versa? In my case, my vertigo is not triggered when I am in airplanes or helicopters— just in buildings. How many of your hot buttons are triggered by certain people but not by everyone you work with? Knowing you can successfully manage the hot button in one situation means that you can learn to manage it in the triggering situation as well.

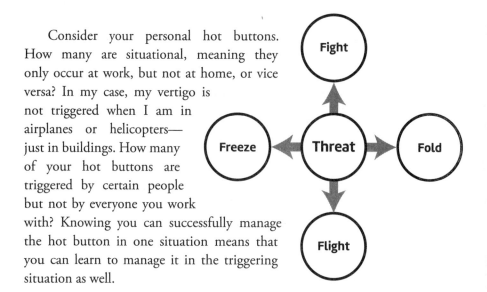

Do You Fight or Run Away?

When your amygdala fires, it triggers four possible responses (sometimes in combination). They are fight, flight, freeze, or fold. It may feel like a cascade effect, where a threat triggers your amygdala, resulting in the "deer in headlights" moment (freeze), while your limbic system and body decide which of the other reactions to implement in that instant.

While each of us will experience emotional hijacks at work, my guess is these rarely end in physical combat (fight) or tying the laces on your Nikes before fleeing for the parking lot (flight). The trigger can be situational, based on location and the person concerned. Think about it (with your neocortex, please). When challenging feedback is delivered by your Ally, my guess is that you are more prepared to consider that feedback than if it's provided by a Rival or Adversary.

A meeting with your boss may be more stressful than a meeting with a member of your team. However, for the team member, receiving feedback from you, their boss, can trigger a hijack in them. In this feedback example, the employee focuses on the threat from you, the boss (am I going to be fired, how will this impact my bonus . . . all imagined threats and all too real to the amygdala), rather than the message being delivered, or the work at hand. Memory, planning, and creativity go out the window, leaving people to resort to old habits, no matter how unsuitable these reactions are for addressing the current challenge.

As leaders, project managers, or subject matter experts within a team, we sometimes overlook the fact that we can trigger others, simply by virtue of our position in the organization. When you carry a title (formal or informal), the power to influence someone's career prospects or bonus payout can trigger a hijack in them. Where you're the expert to whom others have to go for input—chances are their amygdalas will be on hyper-alert when around you. Think back to the team I described earlier, stuck in the threat-react-threat-react loop. Effecting change and breaking this cycle requires each person to consciously and subconsiously act in a way to soothe their amygdala (and yours). Pay attention to your personal fight-or-flight responses (self-awareness) and remain vigilant to the reactions of others around you (social awareness).

Hijacked

I often ask my workshop participants what each emotional hijack looks like in an office environment.

Participants use the following words to describe the *fight* response:

- *Being argumentative, using inappropriate language, raising of voices.*
- *Jumping to conclusions, making assumptions and stating them as fact.*
- *Exhibiting hostile body language—rolling of eyes, banging on the table, aggressive or intimidating behavior, getting in someone's personal space.*
- *Talking behind others' backs—badmouthing someone else or another team.*

And here is how they describe the *flight* response:

- *Shutting down—"I stop contributing to the conversation."*
- *Ignoring others' toxic behaviors, or the issue at hand, for fear of making it worse.*
- *Contradicting ourselves—"I say one thing while thinking the opposite (yes when I should say no)."*
- *"We no longer talk about the important topics, silence has become the norm. We still see the elephant in the room but choose not to call it out. We ignore it."*

The third response we discuss is the *freeze* response. Participants describe it in this way:

- *"I was giving a major presentation to a new client. I hadn't realized how nervous I was until the CEO asked a challenging question. I froze. I knew the answer, but I just couldn't think of it or find the words. I felt so stupid!"*
- *"It feels like I am the proverbial deer in the headlights, where I literally feel paralyzed by the moment."*

The *fold* response is a little more challenging. New managers describe the fold response as one they may experience when they have to deliver tough feedback:

- *"There is one manager in our office who is so aggressive. When he starts on one of his rants, we all stop contributing. It isn't worth raising questions or concerns, even when we are right; he just won't listen. Of course when the project doesn't move ahead and we hit one of the roadblocks we could see, he gets worse and wonders why no one warned him."*
- *"I had to give feedback to a member of my team. They started to get upset and I heard myself telling them that it was no big deal and to let it pass. I did it to avoid the conflict that might have followed. But it was a big deal. They needed to hear the feedback and I undermined myself and the message I needed to deliver in that moment."*
- *"I think of our project review meetings where we all report our 'green,' on-target results even though we may be aware of delays that may impact the project. We report 'green' to keep our boss happy and to avoid the inevitable frustration and anger he displays when things aren't running smoothly."*

If you could learn to keep your amygdala from hijacking your thinking mind in those moments of emotional complexity, you would have more power at your disposal to make better decisions and to respond effectively to your Rival and Adversary relationships.

Heed the Warning Signs

We don't go a day without having at least some degree of a hijack. We are in a perpetual trigger-react-trigger-react loop *unless* we apply new skills and knowledge to break the cycle.

Every time your amygdala fires, chemicals are released into your bloodstream and body. Even if a full-blown hijack doesn't occur, these chemicals remain for a period of time and build up every time a threat triggers a reaction. This state of heightened emotion continues to the point where the final straw breaks the camel's back, resulting in an outburst (or the shutdown) which can seem out of proportion to the most recent trigger.

Ultimately, it is possible to simply be in the wrong place at the wrong time. Let me give you an example of what I mean. You leave the house to drive to work. Running a few minutes late, you realize the fuel tank is on empty. The first mini-hijack is triggered. You fill up and pull out onto the highway only to have a car cut in front of you, causing you to brake suddenly. The driver behind (who can't see what has happened) lays on his horn, and you are now frustrated at the driver in front of you as well as the one behind you. Hijack number 2.

You get to the office (late) and your usual parking space is taken, so you end up having to walk from the far corner of the lot. Hijack number 3. You finally get to your desk and power up your computer, which promptly freezes. Hijack number 4. You decide to grab a coffee, only to find that the last person left the machine empty. Hijack number 5.

It is at this moment that a colleague appears and asks if "you could just . . ." at which point Hijack number 6 sends you over the edge, and you respond to this innocent bystander with the full force of six hijacks! She never knew what hit her.

The good news is that we all come with a built-in system that provides warning signs of an impending hijack, *if* we choose to pay attention. Ignoring those warning signs is what puts us at risk. The key is, can you see, feel, or recognize the signs early enough to do something about them before they become toxic?

Those warning signs may include:
- Sweaty palms.
- Changes in your breathing.
- Feeling flushed.

- An increase in your heart rate.
- Butterflies or knots in your stomach.

When someone asks you, "Are you OK?" and comments, "You don't seem yourself," pay attention. Don't brush it off. Hear the feedback and assess what it is you are doing or not doing that causes others to ask how you are. Sometimes it is easier for others to see our rising stress levels before we do, and their observation can bring us back from the edge.

Disarming a Hijack

There are a number of strategies you can adopt in order to reduce, and potentially prevent, an amygdala hijack. Emotional intelligence means managing the triggers, not just managing the effects of the triggers.

This is where self-management and relationship management come into play. These strategies may seem simple, but they're well researched, time-tested, and very effective. If you know you are entering a stressful situation (for example, a presentation to two hundred people), applying these tactics *before* you walk on stage will increase your chances of a successful outcome. You don't have to wait for the hijack to occur!

In elementary school, we are taught simple (but effective) tactics for dealing with clothing on fire—stop, drop, and roll. By applying these tactics to your emotions, you might just save your reputation and relationships at work.

Stop. This is about getting out of the way, effectively stopping the path to your default behavior in time for you to increase your effectiveness in the moment. The point is to disengage so you can re-engage more powerfully. Remove yourself from the immediate trigger, whether by creating a physical or mental distance. You want to manage the situation and conversation so you can speak your truth, effectively add value, say no when you need to say no, and say yes when you need to say yes.

Tactics include:
- Count to 10.
- Take a break.
- Go for a walk.

Drop. Our brains require 20 percent of the oxygen in our bodies. This is dedicated to basic functions first and, if available, for higher-level needs, such as complex thought, problem solving, and articulating a point of view. During a hijack, blood and oxygen are shunted away from our brain to the main parts of our body to prepare for fight or flight. With a focus on breathing, we return a higher level of oxygen to the brain so it gains greater capacity to function. However, it's not just about taking deep breaths. It is about applying a level of deliberate thought into your breathing. The increased awareness of your breathing stimulates the thinking mind to soothe and cover the effects of your amygdala. You can't think fast and breathe slow!

Tactics include:

- Breathe slowly and deeply.
- Breathe in through your nose and out through your mouth.
- Visualize success, or something or someone that calms you down.

Roll. To override your amygdala, your emotional center, your neocortex needs information; it needs to roll with the punches. Since the limbic system isn't capable of complex thought, you need to re-engage the neocortex by asking questions and seeking more information.

Tactics include:

- Ask yourself, "Why would a rational human being think this of me? Do this to me? Say this about me?"
- Remain curious and test your assumptions for accuracy. Ask open-ended questions. Explain your thinking. Gain feedback from others, not just your Allies but your critics as well.
- Explore your role and contribution to the situation. You have played a part in the quality (or lack thereof) of each interaction and relationship. Take ownership and accountability.

Developing a New Approach

Choosing to build your emotional intelligence is no different from learning any other skill. Your brain grows new connections and pathways every time you practice a new skill, taking you from apprentice to mastery.

Think about the last time you learned something new. Chances are you were initially awkward and only occasionally successful. Over time, your confidence and skill level increased until you could perform the skill with little conscious thought. It is practice, and more importantly the concept of guided practice, that will ensure the neural pathways you are developing are the right habits. Emotional intelligence can be learned and developed.

The latest research has shown that mental practice, visualizing a situation and mentally rehearsing a successful outcome, works as well as *actually* doing it, at least in the early stages of learning. The brain does not differentiate between the two. Of course, if muscle memory is required (such as in a sport), then at some point you will have to get out of the armchair to raise your skills.

This is also true of your interactions with others: thinking through a tough conversation with a coworker may help you more effectively guide that conversation.

Taking Off Your Shoes

Earlier, I talked about developing empathy by putting yourself in the shoes of the other person. In order to do so, you first have to be prepared to take your own shoes off!

• • •

"Do not wait for leaders; do it alone, person to person."

—MOTHER TERESA

• • •

The challenge we face in understanding the other's position before sharing our own is that we try to do this while holding on to our own story and perspective. Seeking to understand another's perspective and putting yourself in his or her shoes allows you to:

• Describe your perspective and expectations in his words, from his point of view.
• "Try on" her perspective and make it your own.
• Choose to meet halfway and combine both of your points of view.
• Create a new perspective that neither of you had considered.

When we start with a "me-first" perspective, we tend to try to persuade others by adding more data and facts, talking louder, or simply using authority to convince the other person. These approaches may force an outcome that meets *your* needs, but it will likely result in more conflict down the road. A more effective approach to influencing others is to first understand their perspective and build from that point.

Here is one pragmatic piece of advice when it comes to "seeking first to understand": someone has to go first. If you are working with someone who has read this book or Stephen Covey's *7 Habits of Extraordinary People,* you will understand that you can't both "seek to understand," one of you has to express your perspective first and build from that point. If you are sharing first, make sure you offer your point of view in a way that invites discussion and clarification.

● ● ●

"Neurons that fire together stay together.
Neurons that are no longer in synch no longer link."

—ADAPTED FROM

DONALD HEBBS

● ● ●

The Impact of Understanding

Emotional intelligence reaffirms that we are, as humans, social creatures. We need to feel social connections with others, where we feel heard and valued and have a sense that others care about us.

When individual relationships or organizational cultures prevent this through toxic behaviors such as intimidation, isolation, or aggressive behavior, the brain creates an emergency stop, making it harder for us to think and behave productively.

Since success at work is determined by our ability to achieve results with others, applying emotional intelligence is critical. Trying to excuse poor choices by saying, "This is just the way I am" or "I had no choice; he was being nasty to me" does not work.

You can choose to react differently; it may take practice and time, but it can be done.

The mindset (and emotion) you carry about others has an impact on the people who work alongside you. When you have a negative impression of someone, you'll look for mistakes and other examples to support your perspective (the case for the prosecution).

On the other hand, when you have a positive perspective of your team, people tend to respond in a way that supports this belief, a self-fulfilling approach that builds confidence.

Having or being an Ally doesn't mean that you are naïve or that you over-indulge others. It doesn't mean you unnecessarily protect others from every threat in the workplace either, (for example, always volunteering to give the group presentation). A healthy approach allows for informed risk-taking and making mistakes, which are treated as learning opportunities rather than reasons for punishment.

Building an organizational culture based on cultivating winning relationships will reduce the perceived threats identified by your reptile brain. Having an Ally reduces your stress level as you tackle the challenges of new tasks. An Ally provides the safety net that empowers action.

Intentionally role-modeling Ally behaviors means that you provide the appropriate support and challenge. Teamwork based on an Ally mindset has a direct impact on the ability of the team to produce results.

Developing an Emotionally Intelligent You

Applying the concepts and skills associated with emotional intelligence is a choice. Old reptiles can learn new tricks. Whatever stage of your career or life, you can make an immediate application to your interactions with others.

We're about to shift from theory to practice, from concepts to action. Self-awareness is the first step in effecting change in your relationship with yourself and with others.

Relationship Revelations

- Emotions drive our behavior, which impacts our performance and relationship with others.
- There are four domains of emotional intelligence:
    o Self-awareness
    o Self-management
    o Social awareness
    o Relationship management
- The competencies and skills of emotional intelligence can be learned and developed at any time, with conscious and deliberate effort.

Your Relationship Responsibilities

1. Select a Rival or Adversary in your career. Which reaction do they trigger in you?
   Fight—Flight—Freeze—Fold
    o How would you describe this person's potential for future success?
    o How do you behave toward, or talk about, this person?
2. What symptoms do you experience when you are stressed and about to hijack?
3. Reflect on a time when you spoke or acted impulsively and later wished you had not. What was the impact on your reputation and on your ability to effectively work together?
4. What are the elephants in the room that are not being discussed but should be? What is the cost of that silence to your relationship and to your ability to effectively work together?

For more practical resources, go to www.CultivateTheBook.com.

generations at work

The children now love luxury. They have bad manners, contempt for authority; they show disrespect for adults, and love to talk rather than work or exercise. They no longer rise when adults enter the room. They contradict their parents, chatter in front of company, gobble down food at the table and intimidate their teachers.

I often use this quote to open my program on generations at work. We ask participants to guess when it was written . . . invariably no one guesses just how old this quote is. (It's from Socrates, who lived from 469 to 399 BC!)

I'll be honest. This subject frustrates me. People love to stereotype, as with gender differences or body language. (Sometimes you cross your arms because the room is cold, not because you're being defensive!) Much of the complaining about the "youth of today" is based on ignorance, and that goes for some young people's accusation that "nobody understands us."

Different values, different ideas, different ways of communicating, and different generations have always existed in the workplace. So, why is this becoming more of a problem now?

Let's change the conversation from birth date to "work date"—the time and place someone enters the workforce. If we change the focus from birth date, and instead take a look at the culture of the workforce when they enter, maybe this can help break down the perceived barriers. Even then, we must resist the temptation to "file" someone in a generational folder, or we'll miss opportunities to listen and grow.

Since I deal with these issues a lot and am somewhere between "old" and "young," trust me when I say we all need to let go of generational stereotypes and cultivate deeper understanding. No matter where you are on the age spectrum, we can all grow.

An Unprecedented Workforce

For the first time in history, there are four distinct generations in the workforce, all with their own perspectives, styles, and expectations. It is projected that in the year 2020, we will have five generations working together. Since this diverse workforce can have a significant impact on your success, we need to take a deeper look at the ramifications of having many generations working together.

Here's an example of just one facet of the differences of the work culture that influenced my family: my grandfather entered the workforce in the 1930s, when it was the norm to stay with a company, and industry, throughout one's entire career. My father (who entered the workforce in the 1960s) also expected to stick with one industry, but he understood that geographical locations and areas of expertise and responsibilities might change.

Contrast this with my career, in four diverse industries, on four continents, in twenty countries. Not only did I expect change, I looked forward to the possibilities. In each case, the mindset was based on the workplace culture, not age of the worker. OK, I will share: I entered the workforce in the late 1980s. There, I said it.

There are also differences based on industry, although the lines are blurring. Early in my career, banking was done on the golf course. Offices were walled off. The relationship aspect was off the radar. Compare that with relational ecosystem at Google. Can you imagine a game room at a bank?

Think of how generational differences, in terms of work worldview, might affect misunderstandings, high employee turnover, difficulty in attracting employees, and the challenge in gaining employee commitment. Understanding each other, including the era in which we were brought up, can be an important element for accomplishing workplace goals and cultivating winning relationships.

In a way, the how, and where, work gets done changes with each generation. Reflect on your experience; my guess is that the way of work for you is different than it was ten years ago. My grandfather lived in a time of a manufacturing and hierarchical approach to managing work. My father and I saw the economy and work move from manufacturing to service industries, which required a different approach and different structures.

As I look forward to the work environment my sons will enter, it is the knowledge economy. In my experience, young people are not "slackers." The amount of knowledge most carry, and their approach to acquiring knowledge, is amazingly different from prior generations. I see this with my own children when I quiz them about current affairs or try to stump them with a pop quiz. If they don't know the answer, then the Internet is only a click away. It's not what you know right now (which my grandfather had to rely upon), but also about knowing how to find the answer.

Here's one last thought before we move on: remember that you—whether as a parent, aunt, uncle, or other extended family member—had a hand in raising the "youth of today." If they aren't meeting your expectations, who is to blame? And for the "youth of today," I want to remind you that you will, one day, be the "adults that the children will be disrespectful toward." Be careful what you wish for.

When it comes to the workplace, one underlying fact has not changed and never will: we all want to be heard and treated with respect.

What Is a Generation?

This term is a reference to an amount of years, roughly thirty years among humans, accepted as the average period between the birth of parents and the birth of their offspring. It is typically used to describe the gap between parents and their children, or members linked through shared life experiences in their formative years. *Generation* can refer to a group of individuals, most of whom are the same approximate age, who share similar ideas, problems, and attitudes.

In the workplace, each individual has his or her own "generational personality": the attitudes, values, and work style shaped by the headlines of the times, politics, economics, places, popular culture, and events that surround them.

The four most common labels for the four current generations are Traditionalists, Baby Boomers, Generation X, and Millennials/ Generation Y. Traditionalists represent those individuals born between 1922 and 1945. The Baby Boomers span the years 1946 through 1964. Generation X includes those individuals born between 1965 and 1980, and Generation Y, or the Millennials, span the years 1981 through 2000. According to a May 2011 US labor force survey of 153 million people, the percentage of individuals in the workforce from each of the four generations was as follows:

Traditionalists:	4.7%	7 million
Baby Boomers:	38.6%	59 million
Generation X:	32.4%	49 million
Generation Y/Millennials:	24.7%	38 million

There is also an important group known as *Cuspers*. These are people who were born in the three-to-five-year period that overlaps two generations. Cuspers might identify with more than one generation, since their birth years fall near the beginning or end of a given range of years. Some identify with two generations and have characteristics of both generations. For example, someone born between 1940 and 1951 might consider him- or herself to be both a Traditionalist and a Baby Boomer. They may therefore have a strong work ethic, yet be eager to challenge the status quo. Cuspers often act as "translators," or mediators, for different generations, since they have the ability to take in a broader generational perspective.

A Brief Introduction to Each of the Four Generations

Let me clarify here, so you don't think I'm contradicting myself. It's important to have some background on the times these generations entered the workforce. These are generalizations that, because of my background, reflect the experience of the so-called western world.

I attended a workshop on generations at work with one of my clients. We were both curious to see what the facilitator had to say. Unfortunately, it did not go well. What the facilitator seemed to fail to realize was that the experiences that had shaped my generation and those of the four other international participants were not the same as those experienced by those who grew up in the United States. My US colleague was mortified by some of the sweeping generalizations that were made. In my mind, it simply served to reinforce that stereotypes are a no-win situation. Even my approach of moving away from birth date to starting work date still misses many of the subtle nuances when it comes to working with anyone, no matter their age, generation, or nationality.

Taking time to learn about different perspectives will enhance the growth of our relationships. So here's the disclaimer: the way to really understand someone, and build a relationship, is to communicate directly with him or her on an individual basis. By all means use the stereotypes as a basis from which to build, but treat them lightly, as hypotheses to be tested, rather than absolutes that will hold true. Hopefully the information below can spark some illuminating conversations.

The Traditionalist/WWII Generation was brought up during a tough economic time. They are sometimes referred to as the Loyal Generation. They were raised with a strict regimen at home and in school. They tend to value job security and hold deep respect for authority. Because of war rationing and difficulties in their formative years, they are known to be frugal and hardworking. They are usually reliable, loyal employees. Their beliefs about the importance of work and of meeting obligations define their careers. They believe in paying cash rather than using credit. They are very different from their children's generation, the Baby Boomers.

The Baby Boomer Generation grew up during times of economic and educational growth and is sometimes referred to as the Loved Generation. They attended school in a traditional system and had rigorous programs available to them. As they developed into young adults, they faced major social upheaval and change. They bucked the system of traditional gender roles, as scores of women entered the workforce. This generation worked hard and earned well. They embraced the value of sacrifice to get ahead. That sacrifice made them loyal to their employees and colleagues.

They differed from their parents' generation in that their financial philosophy was to buy now and pay later. With the rise of consumerism and two-income families, the divorce rate grew.

Generation X consists of the children of the Baby Boomers and has been nicknamed the Lost Generation. They were latchkey children who watched their parents forge a new work environment. They are said to have inherited the "social debris" of the Boomers, with self-absorbed, often divorced parents, which resulted in single-parent, single-income families that had difficulties paying their expenses in the face of a growing national debt and failed corporations.

Accordingly, they are more financially conservative, having learned from their parents' mistakes. Many saw their workaholic parents being laid off from jobs to which they were extremely loyal. Generation X-ers have learned that there's no such thing as job security. They were the first generation to grow up with computer technology. They care more about productivity than they do about the number of hours they spend on the job.

The Millennials (also known as Generation Y) are the most educated, technologically sophisticated generation ever. For this reason, they've been tagged the Linked Generation. They grew up in a world of computers, the Internet, and cell phones—they are entrenched in technology. They multitask and bore easily. They understand how to leverage new technology better than any generation before them. Millennials saw unprecedented events such as the Oklahoma City bombing, the Columbine High School massacre, and September 11, 2001. Being exposed to such fear and lack of security has caused them to value job satisfaction, security, and opportunity for advancement as priorities over financial compensation. They aren't as concerned about saving as the previous generation. They value a balanced lifestyle. Their motto could be "Earn it, spend it."

Stereotypes and Generalizations

Stereotypes prejudge a person's abilities, skills, and personality based on unfair and/or inaccurate assumptions that may relate to racial, physical, or cultural traits. The following are some examples of stereotypes in each of the four generational categories:

Traditionalists: Oftentimes would rather figure out a problem or investigate a process on their own. In response to this behavior, others may assume, *"He/she is not a team player."*

Baby Boomers: Value being a team player, love meetings. In response, others may say, *"Yes, let's have another meeting and be sure to include a group hug!"*

Generation Xers: Tend to be more cynical, skeptical, and less idealistic. In frustration, others may misinterpret their search for authenticity and say something like, *"He/she questions and challenges everything!"*

Millennials: Communication revolves around the Internet and cell phones. In response, others may assume, *"He/she doesn't know how to communicate verbally."*

Understanding Generations

Once again, the references below are intended to increase your understanding and better prepare you for thoughtful interactions, not generalize or label people. We're looking for "aha!" moments, where relationships go to the next level.

To the Traditionalist, key relationships are those where expectations are made clear. Traditionalists prefer not to be rushed and may work best with coworkers who give them ample time to deliver. Traditionalists appreciate communication in the form of memos and one-on-one interactions. Because they tend to stay with a company for years, Traditionalists work better with those who value their expertise and knowledge of the company history. Traditionalists also enjoy being called upon to mentor others.

Since Traditionalists believe that one moves up the ladder through hard work and perseverance, they don't believe in shortcuts—not even in the development of professional relationships. To Traditionalists, strong relationships take time and are developed over a period of years. An effective relationship is one in which their experience and expertise are appreciated. Traditionalists seek relationships built on formality, where respect and honor are valued and displayed.

To the Baby Boomer, the best working relationships are those in which there is a mix of personal and professional—Baby Boomers like having "connection" in the workplace. They also prefer face-to-face communication over electronic messaging. Boomers strive for a team approach and work best with those who will ask for their input.

The Baby Boomers are also open-minded and like to be thought of as up to date. They are always learning and will pursue professional relationships that foster their desire to know more and do their best. Relationships with those who can serve as coaches are especially valuable for a Boomer. Boomers look for opportunities to work with others, especially in collaborative ways. They seek out opportunities to meet in person and strengthen their relationships.

Generation X coworkers enjoy those who like to have as much fun as they do. They prefer flexible work hours, an informal work environment, and a sense of freedom in the workplace. Gen X-ers tend to avoid negative workplace politics, so they look for working relationships where these are left out. Gen X-ers aren't afraid to ask questions, even of those in authority, and they value working with those who encourage questioning. Unlike Traditionalists, they don't get too concerned with hierarchy.

The Gen X-er wants to maintain a balance between work and family and will seek out relationships that support those goals. Members of this generation especially look for relationships where they can have direct and immediate communication, where others ask open-ended questions of them. Having an entrepreneurial spirit, they prefer informal meetings and a casual approach to the development of professional relationships.

Millennials are able to work more easily with any of the other generations because they have the can-do attitude of a Traditionalist, the teamwork ethic of a Boomer, and the technological savvy of the Gen X-er. Millennials respond well to being mentored by older, more seasoned professionals, so they share a particular kinship with Traditionalists.

Millennials want to do meaningful work, and they seek to develop relationships with creative, bright individuals who share that desire. Millennials like developing relationships via social networking, such as Facebook and Twitter. They tend to get frustrated with bureaucracy and what might be perceived as unnecessary rules that slow down work.

Building Bridges

Without over-generalizing (please don't make me write another disclaimer!), to create an Ally relationship with someone from a different generation, the following are some approaches to remember for each generation.

When approaching a Traditionalist:

- Words and tone of voice should be respectful—with good grammar, clear diction, and no slang or profanity.
- Language should be a bit formal, and the message should relate to company history and long-term goals.
- Since Traditionalists value relationships that have been built over time, arrange for face-to-face encounters rather than communication via email or texting.

When approaching a Baby Boomer:

- Be sure your conversation is more relational, perhaps over coffee or lunch. Boomers tend to see relationship and business results as intertwined.
- Ask about mutual interests (e.g., "How is your son doing in college?").
- Make the conversation participative by getting the other's input, and link the message to the team or individual vision, mission, and values.

When approaching a Generation X-er:

- Don't waste the person's time.

- Be direct and straightforward.
- Avoid corporate-speak.
- Send an email or leave a voicemail that states clearly what you want, how it will serve the Generation X-er, and when you want it.

When approaching a Millennial:
- Be positive.
- Leverage technology; don't be afraid to use social media to make the initial contact.
- Tie the message to the Millennial's personal goals or to the goals the whole team is working toward.
- Don't be condescending.
- Avoid cynicism and sarcasm.

Cultivating Multigenerational Relationships

No matter what generation an individual is from, there will always be differences in his or her individual personality and work style. I often refer to the generational differences as straws in the wind. You can't see the wind, yet you can observe the way in which it makes the straws bend. They serve as clues. Likewise, generational information serves as clues to help you engage in more rewarding ways with each person based on who they are—a unique human being.

CHAPTER 12

why relationships turn sour

Assumptions are the termites of relationships.

« HENRY WINKLER »

Why do we experience toxic relationships? Why do apparently solid relationships turn sour? In my experience, most of us have not had opportunities to learn how to build productive working relationships. The assumption is that we are all grown-ups and can work it out as we go along in the School of Hard Knocks.

At some point we will all feel let down, and we will make mistakes. Whatever the trigger, something will happen to change your relationship equilibrium. When you are disappointed by the actions (or inactions) of another, before you set your phaser to "stun," ask yourself why you are disappointed. Did you actually articulate your expectations? If the answer is no, there is culpable negligence on your part.

Relationship Workout
The gap between knowing what we should do and having the discipline to actually follow through can be wide. Those who know me understand that I'm an aspiring athlete, but not always a *perspiring* athlete. . . . There was always a good reason (excuse) why I couldn't get to the gym—now, later today, or at any other time. To date, the only visible side effect of my reluctance to exercise had been the need to buy a larger skirt size than I wore in my twenties. The reality is that when it comes to my health, the only person who can make a difference is me, and the time to take action is today. By the way, before you consider me a complete hypocrite, I am pleased to share that I completed a sprint triathlon this year and am now a regular visitor to a local gym!

Composting Connections
Ineffective relationships don't just "happen" by chance. When we ignore the warning signs in our professional relationships, it is at our own peril. Essentially, relationships turn sour or breakdown when we don't:

- **See.** We stop paying attention or are simply ignorant of the warning signs. For many, the concept of actively discussing relationships comes under the heading of *touchy feely.* We see an assumption, especially with senior leaders, "You've been at this long enough . . . work it out."
- **Listen.** If we do see the warning signs, we fail to prioritize the need, telling ourselves, "I'll get to it tomorrow." We choose to

ignore the warning signs and hope that the situation will resolve itself on its own without the need for intervention.

• **Act.** The final failure is that we don't take action, or worse, we take action without deliberate forethought, which escalates the situation. In this case, we see the warning signs, we recognize the need to act, and we may even have created a plan, but we fail to execute it effectively.

Taking rather than giving. If you have been taking from the "relationship bank account" without making deposits, at some point you'll be overdrawn. A true Ally relationship doesn't keep score, and if you are only doing something because you expect something in return, don't be surprised when things break down.

Forgetting to be present. The most common frustration I hear about relationship-building involves multitasking. We are all guilty of it—checking email while we are on the phone, not actively listening during a conversation. These all send the clear message: "You are not important." If you want to avoid any possibility of this, switch off the computer screen, turn away from the distractions, or, if necessary, signal the fact that you are in the middle of something and schedule time when you can focus. Email can wait. People can't. Consider speaking up if you can't give your full attention and say the following:

I can see this is important to you, and I want to ensure you have my full attention. Right now I have to finish this report/go to a meeting in five minutes/reply to this urgent customer email. Can we please meet at 2:00 p.m. to discuss this further?

This sends a powerful message of commitment to the relationship. Often, instead of taking the lead and signaling our needs, we allow the unexpected interruption, while continuing to think about the work at hand. Nobody wins.

Gossip. When I ask participants if they've spoken to the person they are struggling with, invariably I get a shocked look, followed by a swift no. But when I ask if they've talked about their frustrations with someone else, I get a sheepish yes. Gossip can be good,[11] as a recent research article highlighted; it can actually help build relationships across a team or organization—when the gossip is perceived to be beneficial, to check facts, to increase learning, or undertaken for positive reasons with good intent. However when gossip is designed to undermine others, then it's unhealthy.

By all means, leverage your Ally relationships to prepare for the tough conversations (you know your Ally won't be sharing the information on the corporate grapevine). However, don't be sucked into break room gossip or water cooler conversations.

Breaking commitments. Things will crop up and get in the way of genuine commitments. When this happens, pick up the phone or walk over to the desk and let the parties know you need an extension or are no longer able to assist. If you let your Ally down, you could spend months rebuilding trust, all for the lack of a quick conversation.

Failure to apologize, quickly and sincerely. You are going to make mistakes. When you do, step up quickly and apologize sincerely. Ignore the temptation to tell white lies or minimize the impact you've had on others.

> *Building an effective network of relationships requires a 360° perspective.*

Selective relationship building. If you are focused only on the "right" connections, your style will come across as inauthentic. We've worked with many leaders who, when they analyze their 360° relationship map, discover their relationships are skewed in one direction (usually up) and are not representative across the organization. They put a lot of energy into cultivating relationships with those with the right title and seniority, but devote less care and attention to those elsewhere. Building an effective network requires a 360° perspective, within your industry and outside of it.

Conflict becomes personal. Disagreements are to be expected, if not encouraged, in a healthy team. Effective conflict increases candor and debate—highlighting potential risks, challenging key assumptions, and increasing understanding. When the conflict becomes personal ("That's a stupid idea"), value is destroyed and learning stops.

Office politics. We all know leaders who play office politics like a pro. There are also those who play the relationship card to call in favors from others but rarely reciprocate. Achieving results sometimes requires an "ask," but hidden agendas will come to light.

Taking Allies for granted. Care and feeding of Ally relationships need not be time consuming. A quick phone call or handwritten note every few months can be sufficient. Get in the habit of sending two of these a week and in a year you'll connect with more than one hundred people in your network.

Being an imposter. If you are an Ally, you need to be prepared to step forward and defend your Ally, especially in difficult times. One moment of hesitation and all will be lost.

Forgetting the four questions. Earlier in the book, we outlined four questions we're always asking ourselves, consciously and subconsciously, in each relationship:

1. Can I count on you?
2. Can I depend on you?
3. Do I care about you?
4. Do I trust you?

Lose sight of these questions about colleagues, and about how they view you, and the health of your working relationships will decline.

Reality Check

Recognize that not all relationships will start (or finish) as Allies. In effecting change in your relationships, you should expect the unexpected. There will be times when things transform quickly; there will also be times when a relationship that seems to be making progress suddenly takes a step backward. It is at these times you will need to apply your emotional intelligence skills and be resilient. I encourage you to stay in the game and, if necessary, change your game.

Relationship Revelations

- Relationships turn sour or breakdown when we
    - Stop paying attention and ignore the warning signs.
    - See the warning signs but fail to prioritize the urgency for change.
    - See the warning signs and prioritize the need for change but fail to take action.
- When relationships turn sour, start first by looking at how you contributed to the declining health of the relationship.
- Most relationships can be nursed back to health if you take the appropriate action.

Your Relationship Responsibilities

Identify two situations in which a relationship you considered to be an Ally or Supporter changed and you started to experience Rival or Adversarial behavior.

- What happened and why do you think it happened?
- What boundaries or rules of engagement were broken?
- How did you handle the situation?
- How would the other party describe the situation and what happened?

Moving Forward

- What are you trying to achieve? What is your goal?
- What is the other party's goal? What is he or she trying to achieve?
- How was this aligned or misaligned with your goal?
- What are the common goals and shared objectives?
- What would you do differently if this situation were to arise in the future?

For more practical resources, go to www.CultivateTheBook.com.

CHAPTER 13

speaking up: four strategies

You can't stay in your corner of the Forest waiting for others to come to you. You have to go to them sometimes.

« A. A. MILNE, *WINNIE-THE-POOH* »

Thinking about the nature of working relationships is the easy part. While you may be feeling a little overwhelmed by your newfound Relationship Ecosystem™, it will all be for nothing unless you choose to take action. And the best time for you to strengthen your working relationships is next Wednesday. OK, I'm kidding. Today's the day!

What follows are four strategies, and the conversations to support you. As much as you prepare, especially for the tough conversations, the live conversation rarely follows the script you've written.

One leader in my program described how this plays out in professional relationships, using the analogy of a car and bicycle approaching an intersection. It doesn't matter if the bicycle has the right of way or not. If the bicycle is in the blind spot, out of the car's mirror, the *bicycle* needs to yield to ensure a successful outcome.

When applied to professional relationships, it doesn't matter how "right" you are, or how "wrong" you perceive the other person to be—you may need to yield.

But you do have the power to take the first step in letting go of the past (the baggage that may be weighing down the relationship) and initiating the conversations to effect change. Your success depends on it.

Four Relationship Strategies

These strategies are designed to achieve agreement about how you will work together effectively and to clear up any past misunderstandings. The four relationship strategies do not occur in any particular order, though experience has shown the first strategy, Align, is usually the best way to start.

Each strategy includes three specific conversations. The intent is not to have all these conversations at once, or even to have all the conversations every time. Instead, think of them as an à la carte menu.

Essential Qualities of an Ally Mindset

You will recall the essential qualities that support an Ally relationship:
1. Abundance & Generosity
2. Courage & Vulnerability
3. Candor & Debate
4. Action & Accountability

Relationship Strategies

Relationship Focus
- Nurture Allies
- Rally Supporters
- Manage Rivals
- Address Adversaries

BAGGAGE

Relationship Mindset
- Abundance & Generosity
- Courage & Vulnerability
- Candor & Debate
- Actions & Accountability

ALIGN

ADJUST

APPLAUD

Relationship Impact
- Engagement
- Collaboration
- Learning
- Success

The relationship strategies and each conversational tactic require you to have the right mindset initially to ensure success. If you aren't in the right place to start with, you can probably guarantee any conversation will appear insincere and ultimately do damage.

(So if you've skipped to this point in the book . . . now would be an excellent time to read the earlier chapters. This is serious business!)

Relationship Focus — What You Are Trying to Do

As you consider the starting point for each relationship within the Relationship Ecosystem™, your focus is to:

- **Nurture Allies:** It would be easy to assume an Ally relationship can be maintained with little attention, and in some cases this is true. As I think about my network and stakeholders, there are people I would consider Allies and to whom I'm an Ally. Some

I speak with on a daily basis, but with others it may have been many months since we last spoke.

Frequency is not the issue; it's the quality of those interactions. Nurturing an Ally relationship can be as simple as sending a birthday card or leaving a brief phone message. It can be as involved as engaging in daily projects and going the extra mile. The key is not to neglect and to be intentional.

- **Rally Supporters:** Supporters can be both a boon and a burden. In applying the strategies, your goal is to rally your Supporters, strengthening your connection and moving them toward Ally status.
- **Manage Rivals:** With Rivals, the focus is on managing the potential volatility in the relationship. If you can understand your Rival's perspective and anticipate when he or she may be for or against you, it reduces the chance of deterioration toward adversarial behaviors and moves this relationship closer to being a Supporter.
- **Address Adversaries:** As I shared in my own example of working with an Adversary, you cannot simply ignore the issue and hope it goes away. Tolerating Adversary behaviors allows those behaviors to be reinforced and potentially affect others. While the conversations will provide a framework for addressing any Adversaries, my advice is to think carefully before confronting this relationship head on.

Also consider that a more effective approach is to strengthen relationships with your Rivals, Supporters, and Allies, allowing these shifts to influence your Adversary indirectly.

THE FOUR RELATIONSHIP STRATEGIES
Relationship Strategy: ALIGN
When discussing why we don't ALIGN expectations and speak up to ensure we are in agreement, I hear several common reasons, including the fear of being perceived as "soft." Once you have some tools for conversations, you'll find the courage to speak up, in spite of the risk.

FOCUS
- Nurture Allies
- Rally Supporters
- Manage Rivals
- Address Adversaries

BAGGAGE

MINDSET
- Abundance & Generosity
- Courage & Vulnerability
- Candor & Debate
- Actions & Accountability

ALIGN
- Rules of Engagement
- Work Style
- Decisions

ADJUST

APPLAUD

IMPACT
- Engagement
- Collaboration
- Learning
- Success

WHO: This strategy is most suitable for Ally, Supporter, and Rival relationships.

WHEN: Too often, we focus on WHAT needs to be achieved at work, instead of discussing HOW we will work together. Where existing relationships are not strained, or if this is a new stakeholder relationship, then the dialog can start from the center of the diagram model.

HOW: There are three conversations that are part of the ALIGN strategy:

1. Specify the rules of engagement.
2. Address work style.
3. Outline decision making.

Yes, we're being very deliberate here, but there are at least two huge benefits. First, you'll learn new skills, (and yes, this can sometimes feel like going back to elementary school). Secondly, we're training our mind and emotions to pause and consider new ways of acting (and reacting).

- **Conversational Tactic 1—Specify the Rules of Engagement:**
  Three months after leaving the banking industry (a true nine-to-five environment) to join an American telecom firm, I was asked by my coworker, "Why do you keep leaving early?"

  I left the office at five o'clock to catch the six o'clock train from London. It turns out, somewhere in all the new paperwork, I had missed the fact that the working hours at my new company were 9:00 a.m. to 6:00 p.m., allowing an extra hour to work with our American colleagues. I thought I was leaving on time, and my colleagues thought I was leaving early—new rules of engagement that others assumed I knew! It was an easy change to make, once I was made aware of it.

- **Conversational Tactic 2—Understand Work Style:** If the rules of engagement represent the rule book that holds a relationship together, the individual work style of each person influences how those rules are played out in the office. In an Ally relationship, this uniqueness is celebrated.

  Another personal example—I've been married for nearly twenty-five years and consider this my most significant Ally relationship. The differences between our individual personality styles are clear to all who know us. I am the extrovert; I bring ideas, optimism, and enthusiasm. I like to socialize, but don't expect me to bring attention to detail. My husband is the introvert; he brings detail, pragmatism, and a well-planned approach to family and finances. Our strength and teamwork come from these very differences. Together, we are better versions of ourselves.

  I can also attest that during our twenty-five years together we've experienced all four relationship behaviors—Ally, Supporter, Rival, and Adversary—sometimes all on the same day!

  This is important to note—it's the *overarching* relationship dynamic that is most critical. We all have off days—problems arise, and frustration and conflict occur. The damage is done when both players move away from an Ally mindset at the same time.

  Being an Ally means giving the benefit of the doubt, remaining curious, taking the time to inquire about what is happening, and sharing what we need to maintain a healthy dialogue. Only when insights about what's working and what's not have been aired can we set up a relationship for success. In this particular conversational tactic, leveraging tools such as the DISC, MBTI® or other assessments can be useful in providing a common language.

- **Conversational Tactic 3—Agree on Decision Levels:** Nothing seems to cause more friction than a decision that was made where the other party believes they should have been consulted. Having this conversation before an initiative begins brings clarity as to what decisions impact the relationship and how final decisions will be made.

Gaining agreement when working together is easy and ensures that when the tough times hit (and they will) you have a framework to fall back on.

Who Goes There? Ally or Adversary?

Some difficult relationships are not Rivals or Adversaries; they are just different or annoying. I recall facilitating a high-performing team program for a sales organization in a major tech company. Two senior team members were David and Stephen, who had been in conflict with each other for months. The relationship had deteriorated to such an extent that David saw Stephen as his Adversary and treated him as such.

Since they had never discussed their relationship, or the fact that David saw it as adversarial, they were stuck in a behavior loop that was starting to impact others on the team. True to form, the two sat at opposite ends of the table and barely acknowledged each other's presence.

As part of the program, we were utilizing the MBTI® (Myers Briggs Type Indicator) personality profile to better understand the differences within the team and their client relationships. Once the MBTI styles had been discussed and we had completed a number of activities to bring the theory alive, David realized that his colleague was his exact opposite in terms of preferences. They weren't trying to annoy each other on purpose, they both simply "couldn't help it."

As a result of that session, they were able to sit down and discuss strategies for working more effectively together—strategies that were built on common ground—and identify adjustments each could make. This didn't require a personality transplant but took into account the different needs of each person and the overarching goals of the team.

Relationship Strategy: ADJUST

Stuff happens. The ADJUST strategy is vital—reminding others of a previous commitment (during the ALIGN conversation) or as a result of changing priorities.

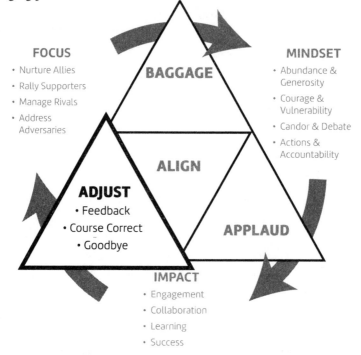

A "first infraction" to the rules of engagement may mean an adjustment conversation is pretty simple: a reminder, an apology, and a commitment to alignment. Where there is a pattern of behavior, or if this conversation doesn't happen immediately, it may require more preparation.

WHO: Ally, Supporter, Rival, Adversary

WHEN: This strategy is used when the commitments made as a result of an ALIGN conversation are not being adhered to on a consistent basis.

WHY: An effective ADJUST conversation allows us to hold each other accountable to the expectations in the ALIGN conversations. We are all human, which means we will make mistakes; we will forget to include others in a discussion and make assumptions.

HOW: The three conversations within ADJUST include:

1. Feedback
2. Course correct
3. Goodbye

An ADJUST conversation avoids assumptions and provides course corrections before new (bad) habits are ingrained.

- **Conversational Tactic 1—Feedback:** The feedback conversation tends to focus on the individual, their approach, and how this may help or hinder success. As an Ally, ensure that the feedback being provided is what someone *needs* to hear (but may not want to hear) and is communicated in a timely manner. A feedback conversation will likely explore alternative courses of action, the learning, and how these can be applied in the future.

- **Conversational Tactic 2—Course Correct:** This conversation may focus more on the process used to collaborate, rather than on the individual. A Course Correct conversation may also be required where priorities and schedules change, necessitating a recalibration of how you will work together.

- **Conversational Tactic 3—Goodbye:** Sometimes the effort to turn around an Adversary or Rival relationship far outweighs the benefits to be gained. Recognize that it will be necessary to say goodbye. On the surface, this sounds like a straightforward tactic—simply stop going to their meetings or stop returning emails. In reality, a Goodbye conversation is challenging.

  This conversation focuses on your exit strategy and how you will work together, in a respectful way, in spite of the ongoing differences. A way needs to be found to work respectfully, to ensure that the team's goals are achieved. Cultivating winning relationships means knowing when to walk toward a relationship and when it is simply best to walk away.

My Boss Is an Adversary

Rich recognized that Scott, his former peer and now his new boss, was an Adversary. He also assumed the feeling was mutual. In meetings, they seemed to disagree on everything.

Empowered by the strategies he'd learned in our program, Rich decided to have a meeting with Scott and asked, "What's going on? We're never on the same page, yet we both want the same thing . . . success!"

His new manager replied, "You come into meetings with strong opinions. You tell us what needs to happen without listening or asking for input."

As they discussed their communication styles, Rich had a huge A HA moment. He realized he was an extrovert—thinking by speaking. When Rich was sharing an opinion, he was simply thinking out loud. His boss was an introvert; he heard the "thinking out loud," as "this is what we are going to do."

Talking about their styles made a huge difference. The arguments went away and the relationship turned around.

Relationship Strategy: BAGGAGE

If your critical relationship is relatively new, it may be sufficient to have an ALIGN conversation. However, if your critical relationship has "history," where trust is eroded or nonexistent, then a BAGGAGE conversation may be need to be unpacked.

WHO: Ally, Supporter, Rival, Adversary

WHEN: The BAGGAGE conversation is designed to clear the air regarding past difficulties that may be preventing you from moving to a healthier position. Once the rules of engagement have been broken, whether founded or unfounded, we will inevitably view others' actions through a negative lens.

The BAGGAGE conversation was named by a client who, following the Cultivating Winning Relationships section of his company's leadership program, took accountability for making changes in two unproductive relationships. He committed to meeting with each individual to move things forward to a more productive level. At our next event, he shared his experience.

With the first relationship, he simply sat down and said, "We need to talk." By his own admission, the conversation that ensued did not go as

FOCUS
- Nurture Allies
- Rally Supporters
- Manage Rivals
- Address Adversaries

BAGGAGE
- Apologize
- Forgive
- Name the Elephant

ALIGN

ADJUST

APPLAUD

MINDSET
- Abundance & Generosity
- Courage & Vulnerability
- Candor & Debate
- Actions & Accountability

IMPACT
- Engagement
- Collaboration
- Learning
- Success

well as he hoped. Reflecting on the experience, he approached the second conversation in a slightly different manner.

He opened with, "We need to have a baggage conversation." This choice of words piqued the curiosity of his colleague, and they were able to have a productive conversation. As he pointed out, you can't hope to create a better future if you can't let go of the past. Spoken like a wise baggage handler!

The phrase *Baggage conversation* resonated for me and the rest of the class, and we've since adopted it to describe the tough conversations you need to have. These conversations will involve some personal risk, namely that the conversation may lead to blame and finger-pointing; however, the risks of not recognizing the obstacles, and not having the courage to call out the past, can be far more damaging.

WHY: A successful BAGGAGE conversation creates a sense of urgency and accountability for resolving the problem. It can also diffuse a pattern of finger-pointing, identifying the source of tension and potential obstacles.

HOW: The three conversations within BAGGAGE are:
1. The apology
2. Forgiveness
3. Name the elephant

A BAGGAGE conversation is particularly pressing when an Ally or Supporter relationship has been damaged in some way.

- **Conversational Tactic 1—The Apology:** When you have crossed a line, repairing the damage means reviewing how you've contributed to the problem—and what you need to do to fix it (not "what the two of you need to do" or "what the other person needs to do"). Fixing a damaged relationship starts with you.

    When you make a mistake (get ready for some brilliant advice . . .), say you are sorry.

    Say it as soon as possible. Don't keep silent, waiting for the right moment. This will only cause any crack in the relationship to become a gaping fissure, making the conversation harder. Say "I apologize" because you mean it.

    One last tip: when and if you are apologizing don't expect the other person to reciprocate in that same conversation. Simply wait and hear the thank you. I know from personal experience that when I have apologized to others for my mistakes, if I am not thoughtful it is to easy to think "Grrrr, she didn't apologize to me for x, y, z," and slip into righteous indignation, which means I go and put my foot in it again. This is about what *you* want to say to the other person. Not what he or she may need to say to you.

- **Conversational Tactic 2—Forgiveness:** Forgiveness is twofold. You may need to forgive others *and* forgive yourself. If an apology isn't warranted, or isn't possible, forgive yourself and let it go. Learn from the situation, and take time out to understand what you can do differently in the future. On the other hand, if you feel the other person has done something to cause the breakdown, you must either forgive them or let it go—chalking it up to human nature. Carrying a chip on your shoulder about a perceived slight made six months ago will not help. Without the ability to forgive others and move on, the following steps will be limited in their success.

- **Conversational Tactic 3—Name the Elephant:** The final conversation in the BAGGAGE section is called *name the elephant.* Sometimes there are challenges outside of the relationship itself that may cause difficulties. For instance, maybe your team goals are simply in conflict and cannot be changed. In this case, it's better to name the elephant (or maybe adopt the elephant) and find a way to work together in spite of it.

In preparing for a BAGGAGE conversation, carefully consider what you want to share. Choosing not to bring up a topic isn't disingenuous if you can let it go. If there are several points of contention in the relationship, then simply pick one for this conversation. To present a laundry list of frustrations will only make the situation worse. As your relationship-building progresses, you can always come back to the other frustrations later.

Relationship Strategy: APPLAUD

The APPLAUD strategy is probably the most critical in maintaining a healthy relationship. In reality, however, it's all too easy to overlook opportunities to celebrate the success of others.

WHO: Ally, Supporter (While I do believe that it is possible to APPLAUD a Rival or an Adversary, I recognize that the opportunities to do so in a genuine way are limited.)

WHEN: Research continually shows that employees value recognition of their contributions, yet when asked, "Have you received praise or recognition in the last seven days?" the vast majority answer in the negative. Think about your own experience—when was the last time someone went out of their way to thank you?

WHY: To acknowledge the value and contribution of others.

HOW: The three conversation tactics that support APPLAUD include:

1. Thank you
2. Celebrate success
3. I am your Ally

As you consider the conversational tactics within this strategy, remember that you can never APPLAUD enough—relationships are never damaged by genuine praise and recognition.

- **Conversational Tactic 1—Thank You:** It's easy to underestimate just how far a simple thank you can go toward cultivating a winning relationship. A personal note can make all the difference in the world, in the way others feel about you, your professional relationship, and the organization. The opportunities to say thank you are plenty: when a colleague puts aside his or her work to help you get a project finished on time, when others provide coaching you need, when a customer (internal or external) makes changes to his or her process to help *you* succeed. Make a point of slowing down to acknowledge others' contributions.

- **Conversational Tactic 2—Celebrate Success:** If the thank you is about acknowledging others' contributions, this conversation is about giving praise to them in a one-to-many environment.

Whether it's leveraging your company's recognition processes, sending notes of appreciation to your Ally's line manager, or nominating him or her for an award, actively seek these opportunities to celebrate others' success. Celebrating success is about being a cheerleader for your Ally to allow others see the value your Ally brings to the team.

Within the HR industry, numerous awards are given to individuals who make a contribution to developing their employees. Within my company, we regularly review the work our clients are undertaking to identify opportunities to nominate them for recognition. It underpins our "abundance & generosity" approach to business and strengthens the working relationship. Beyond that, we simply enjoy it, and you will too.

- **Conversational Tactic 3—I Am Your Ally:** If you have an Ally, or more to the point, if you are one to someone else, tell that person you are his Ally. No, this doesn't have to be awkward! If the person doesn't already know, then you aren't (yet) in an Ally relationship. You don't have to use the exact words, "I am your Ally." Find the language that works for you. Don't hesitate—if you mean it. Telling someone you have his back, confirming you are his Ally, is powerful.

WHO SHOULD YOU TALK TO FIRST?

By now, your mind may be spinning around past encounters, the health of current relationships, and thoughts about what to do next. Through the Relationship Ecosystem™, you have the tools to evaluate the health of your working relationships. You're identifying those relationships that are working for you (your Allies), those that are currently not (Adversaries), and those that may cause you issues in the future (Rivals and Supporters). The next step is to move into thoughtful and deliberate action.

In deciding who to talk with first, and which strategy to adopt, revisit the critical stakeholder list. Focus first on building your Ally relationships. Notice I am suggesting you do not start with an Adversary relationship, even though an Adversary may be causing you the most pain right now. In the mind of the Adversary, for whom cultivating winning relationships is likely not a priority, your attempt to change the way you work together may be dismissed, or may even result in increased adversarial behavior.

This is not about having just one conversation; these simply serve to start the process. It's about the second conversation (and the third and fourth), which determine whether you can strengthen a relationship and move toward becoming an Ally.

Let's get ready to talk.

RELATIONSHIP REVELATIONS
- A relationship mindset and Ally behaviors occur at the intersection of
    o Abundance & Generosity: Share your expertise and time to coach others to success.
    o Courage & Vulnerability: Let your guard down to enable learning.
    o Candor & Debate: Discuss the undiscussables before they become barriers.
    o Action & Accountability: Demonstrate the behaviors of an Ally without fail.
- There are four Relationship Strategies
    o Align
    o Adjust
    o Baggage
    o Applaud
- Cultivating, and maintaining, winning relationships happens one conversation at a time.

CHAPTER 14

your conversational plan

Business is about relationships. Success is about relationships. Leadership is about relationships. Life is about relationships.

« TOMMY SPAULDING, *IT'S NOT JUST WHO YOU KNOW* »

You've decided which relationships need your immediate care and attention. You have identified which of the relationship strategies and conversational tactics are needed. What are you going to say? In creating your conversational plan, even a few minutes of forethought can make all the difference.

If you've ever received feedback that was so vague you wondered what just happened, or at the other end of the scale, received feedback that stung so hard you couldn't think straight, you will know what I mean!

While the template should be customized for your ecosystem, we've found it invaluable to think through a conversation. This chapter is broken into three sections:

1. Before the conversation
2. During the conversation
3. After the conversation

BEFORE THE CONVERSATION

Preparation means knowing what you're going to say and exactly how you'll begin, not winging it once you hear the sound of your own voice. You're speaking with a critical stakeholder in your career after all.

Planning also reduces the *buts*, as in: "*I know I need to talk with Jim, but he's going to think I'm stupid. It will only make things worse.*" Even when we know we should speak up, we hold back. Common reasons (excuses) for not speaking up include:

- Challenging my boss—fear of repercussions or retaliation.
- Follow the pack—everyone else seems to be OK with the situation, I don't want to be different.
- I keep raising the same issues and don't want to be a nag.
- What's the point? He doesn't (or won't) listen to me.
- What's the point? She didn't keep her promise last time. I don't think she can change.
- This is just the way it is. I will just have to put up with it.

If tensions are high, that's all the more reason to create a solid plan. Yes, preparation may lead you to *not* have the conversation now. *Don't let fear substitute for reason.* Think carefully not only about the risks of having the conversation but also about not having it. Should you decide not to speak up, let it be a deliberate choice.

Practice Makes Perfect—Guided Practice Makes Perfect-er

Things can also seem easier in our imagination. When preparing for a critical conversation, don't do so in isolation. If you have an Ally, seek his or her perspective. Consider role-playing the conversation. (Yes, really.) I can guarantee the dialogue will *never* follow the script you have in your head.

You can't control the conversation, but you can control how it begins. By preparing your opening words, you can set the appropriate tone for what follows. Be aware of the amygdala hijack (both yours and theirs) and if the conversation starts to get heated, don't be afraid to call a time out.

You may never find the perfect words or phrases. Do it anyway. Better to start a conversation with 80 percent fluency than to leave the issue to fester until it becomes too difficult to face. Here's something else I've learned: the fact that you thoughtfully prepared will shine through your words and demeanor. Since nonverbal communication can speak louder, the other party will likely notice your intent.

Where should you have these conversations? This is a personal choice. They may need to occur at work, though try to avoid a formal business setting, as this may be misinterpreted as a reprimand. Find a neutral location (especially for Baggage or Adjust conversations), perhaps over a cup of coffee, a walk around the office campus, or in the car on the way back from a meeting.

Relationship Pulse Check

Sometimes a full-blown relationship conversation isn't required. All that is needed is a quick pulse check, an opportunity to identify what may have changed since expectations were discussed. In this case, there are six questions I usually ask:

1. What has been happening for you since we last spoke?
2. What's working well?
3. What's getting in the way of our success?
4. How have I missed your expectations?
5. What have I done to amaze you recently?
6. What is one thing I can do to help ensure your/our success?

Don't press all six questions in one conversation, or it will feel like an interrogation. However, I do try to ensure that over time I'm asking each of these questions on a regular basis with my critical stakeholders.

For my Ally relationships, I may use more of an overt "Let's review the six questions" approach. Building effective working relationships doesn't have to be done in secret—share the script and the process (and give them a copy of this book). When you are on the same page, it becomes much easier to cultivate winning relationships.

Here are some good practices as you enter into your conversations:

- Be purposeful: Before starting a conversation, be certain about what you want to achieve. Know the desired outcome. This will help you to both frame the opening of the conversation and keep it on track.
- Be present: Have the conversation because you want to, not because you feel obligated. Be present during the conversation (i.e., no multitasking), and make sure you allow sufficient time.
- Be clear as to the benefits, both for you and for the other party.
- Empathize, not sympathize. Put yourself in the shoes of the other person. How would you feel in his or her situation? Listen both for what is being said and what remains unspoken.
- Remain curious. Curiosity can help reduce the risk of defensiveness, especially if you are clearing the air and the other person shares his or her frustrations. At this point, you may feel your amygdala fire, asking "Why would a rational person think this?" Remember, *you* started this conversation; it's up to you to manage it.
- Listen. One of the most difficult tasks to do in a conversation is pure listening. While the other person is talking, avoid thinking about what you want to say next. Don't panic if the conversation isn't following your expected "script." Use silence as a powerful tool and provide enough time for the other person to both think through her response and have time to fully express it.
- Validate. Don't assume you are both on the same page in regard to the starting point, or the desired finish. After you have spoken, give the other person a time to share his perspective on what has happened, and ask for his suggestions for moving

forward. Ask clarifying questions to validate and confirm your understanding.

- Agree on next steps. Ensure there are clear next steps, whether these are to continue the conversation or revisit the commitments made, and then follow through.

During the Conversation

Manage your emotions—don't act in the heat of the moment. If you are wound up or tense, wait until you are in a more focused frame of mind. When someone starts to react rather than respond to you, or to react in a way you did not intend, the first step is to clarify your intentions.

Remember, you've been mulling this over for months, but the other person is hearing this for the first time! Feel free to take a break and come back to the conversation. If you've planned the opening of the conversation well, the other party will be able to process your (good) reasons for the discussion. It's about the conversation, not winning.

Relationship Conversation Template

Experience shows that when we have to deliver a tough message, we often waffle on and on instead of getting to what needs to be said. When offering negative feedback, we may soften the message so much that the intent is lost. If you recognize this behavior, give yourself credit for the desire to communicate in a positive way. And also realize that most people are hungry for straight talk. In our leadership programs, we ask group members how they like to have "good news" or "bad news" shared. Without fail, they all say "Just tell me!" Lay out the facts and let the conversation follow.

Position the conversation: The first element is to set up the conversation, to let the other person know what you want to discuss, and to describe the event that occurred. Give the location, time, surrounding details, and events in a way that creates context, helping the other person remember his or her thinking and behavior at the time.

"Fiona, it feels to me as if we have been butting heads recently, **for example, in our meeting yesterday morning when I asked about the report.** *I'm not sure what's causing the problem, but I would like to figure out how to improve the situation. What do you think about how we work together?"*

Ask for permission: Having outlined what you want to discuss, ensure the timing is right; does the other person have the time (and inclination) for this conversation right now? Participants will often ask me, "But what if the answer is no?" My response is that you need to respect the other person's decision and identify an alternative. It may sound something like:

> *"Now may not be the best time, but this is important and I do want to ensure that we can discuss (restate the purpose for the conversation). How about next Tuesday afternoon; what works for you?"*

At this point, you need to make sure the person sees this as a safe, two-way conversation. Empathize with his or her initial response and clearly restate the purpose for the conversation. Include the WIIFT (What's In It For Them) to invest the time and energy. How will it help both of you to achieve your goals?

Describe the behavior: Once you're beginning the conversation, the third element is to describe behaviors of the person involved. This is also the most crucial step, and it is the one most often omitted, probably because actual behaviors can be difficult to identify. The most common mistake is when judgments are communicated using adjectives that describe a *person* but not a person's *actions*.

Give specific examples and provide supporting data. For example, recalling a conversion as, "You did not care about this deadline at all," accuses the person of being uncaring and irresponsible, whereas, "On Monday, you agreed to send me the report by Wednesday" simply states the facts of the situation.

State the impact: The third step is to relay the *impact* the other person's behavior had or any possible consequences if those actions continue—how the person's behavior might affect the organization, coworkers, a program, or their own success.

> *"In the team meeting last week, you interrupted me three times. It really felt like what I had to say was not heard or valued. **I found it frustrating, which meant I stopped listening to the debate and contributing my best efforts.**"*

Share expectations: Rules of engagement for the future are equally important. Yes, people really do plan important conversations this deliberately. Think of the guidelines as training wheels—they keep you from falling over in your meeting!

*"In the team meeting last week you interrupted me three times. It really felt like what I had to say was not heard or valued. I found it frustrating, which meant I stopped listening to the debate and contributing my best efforts. **We don't have to agree, but we do need to understand the different perspectives we bring.**"*

Explore: The final step is asking a question that brings the other person into the conversation and checks for mutual understanding. Everything before this point has been one-way communication, from you to the other person. This is the opportunity for you to open up the dialogue into a two-way conversation.

"Were you aware of this?" or *"What are your thoughts?"* or *"What do you suggest going forward?"*

Pick *one* question . . . and then *shut up*. Wait. Let your partner process what you've said, decide what he or she thinks, and reply. Get comfortable with silence.

Agreement: In bringing the conversation to a close, summarize your understanding of what has been discussed. Confirm next steps. Also take the time to agree on a follow-up process—it may be that you both identify things you wished you had said. Discussing next steps also makes it easier to course correct as necessary, holding each other accountable to the rules of engagement.

Thank you: A sincere expression of thanks, to acknowledge the other person's time and input, is the best way to close this chapter of the conversation.

AFTER THE CONVERSATION:

What the heck just happened? With the right mindset and planning, most of these talks will go well; some may be slightly bumpy. But every conversation deserves reflection. A reflection note can also be completed each time you practice a new skill or behavior; it will help to reinforce your growth.

Use these questions to identify patterns of behavior in order to leverage successes, and reduce the impact of setbacks.

- Exactly what happened, and why do you think it happened in that way? (What are the facts as you see them?)
- How did you behave, think, and feel as it was happening?
- What were the main learning points from this experience?
- What will you do differently as a result of this? (Think about stop doing, start doing, continue doing.)

When things don't go according to plan or others don't reciprocate as you would like, ask yourself "Why would a rational human being do that or say that about me?" This can go a long way toward providing you with choices and alternative explanations rather than the limiting belief that the other person is simply a jerk. More importantly, stick to your commitment to be and behave as an Ally and return to the conversation and relationship another day.

CHAPTER 15

your most important ally

*The most powerful relationship you will ever
have is the relationship with yourself.*

« STEVE MARABOLI, *LIFE, THE TRUTH, AND BEING FREE* »

Let's take a close look at the relationship mindset you apply to . . . yourself. This is the inner Ally, who provides you with courage and insight or, at times, can undermine your self-confidence, causing you to question your own abilities.

Sabotage

When you think of exceptional leaders, their flaws don't come to mind; their strengths do. This isn't because these people were perfect, but their strengths, and the consistency with which they displayed them, outweighed the weaknesses.

When I ask clients and workshop participants to list their own strengths, what makes them exceptional, you can sense the panic in the room. For some reason, it becomes a more difficult exercise to sing our own praises. However, if you can't list your strengths, how can you expect others to acknowledge them?

If you think getting to the next step in your career is out of reach, you won't even apply when an opportunity comes along. Maybe you'd be promoted if you apply; maybe you wouldn't. Either way, it's an occasion for you to learn and grow.

A keynote speaker at a recent conference asked the five hundred attendees to raise their hands if they could paint a picture. Hardly a hand went up. He then went on to say that when he asks the same question of a class of five-year-olds, *every* hand goes up.

A young child isn't worried about whether or not a picture is going to be "good enough." All the child wants to know is whether you want it in crayon, pen, or paint! Yet as adults we start with, "I could try, but it won't be very good." Why is that? Why are we so hard on ourselves?

Inside Out

There are two sides to each of us. There is the "inside out view"—our intent, our perception of who we think we are. Then there's the "outside in view"—the actual impact we have on others, our reputation, and what others experience when working with us. When we allow one perspective to outweigh the other, we become out of balance. We wear a mask to hide our uncertainty or become paralyzed when listening to the internal voice that tells us we aren't good enough.

Consider the following scenarios—have you ever:

- Driven home from work and, without talking to anyone, talked yourself into a bad mood?
- Decided not to apply for a new role because you didn't think you were ready, only to discover later that the hiring manager hoped you would apply (and assumed you were not interested when you didn't)?
- Passed on an opportunity for fear of the possible consequences, only to regret it later?
- Dismissed positive feedback you perceived to be wrong, only to have this limit your opportunities?

Self-talk can be powerful in its ability to build self-confidence, overcome barriers to success, and get us out of danger. However, unhealthy talk also has the ability to paralyze us—to limit our perspective and our options.

- We worry about the future—what might happen, what potential pitfalls we may experience.
- We worry about the past—what we should have said or done.
- We worry about the here and now—being caught out as a fraud, missing an impending deadline, what others think of us.

What's interesting is that when things don't go as planned, most of the stories we tell ourselves are negative. We rarely start by giving ourselves (or the other person) the benefit of the doubt. Don't believe me?

- Imagine you've been working hard on a project for the last few months and have prepared an executive presentation. You are scheduled (for the second time) to deliver that presentation in ten minutes, when you receive a message to say the executive team has canceled your meeting. What is going through your mind?
- A colleague who has missed past deadlines is due to submit a document to you by close of business today. Your phone rings and the caller ID displays this person's name. What are you thinking as you answer the phone?

- You applied for a promotion and have just heard that you didn't get it. Instead, the role went to the newest member of the team. What's going through your mind?

Experience has shown that most of the explanations you consider will assume the worst: that the executives don't know what they are doing, that your project isn't important; that your colleague is about to let you down again and won't have the work done on time; that you aren't good enough and your career has stalled. And we hang onto these negative stories and emotions far longer than any positive ones we may tell ourselves. They can impact our mindset and behavior long after the event has passed.

Only a small percentage of explanations, if any at all, will provide a best case scenario. For example, "The executives have confidence in me and are focused on another priority," "My colleague is calling to say the project is finished early," and "There is another job opportunity, which is perfect for me, just around the corner."

Here's the really tragic part: when all we have are negative stories, we unconsciously create a lackluster action plan. We slow down our effort on the project; we marginalize our coworker; we dust off our résumé and start looking for a new company.

Beliefs and Behaviors

When we allow our negative thoughts to influence our decisions rather than explore alternative points of view, we will take action that limits our potential. We all have our own personal "yes, but" that informs our thought process. What follows are some of the most common themes participants have shared in our programs.

- **Saying Yes When You Mean No**—In an attempt to avoid rocking the boat, we may overcommit and defer to others' judgment. Others may perceive you as pleasant and agreeable, while also misperceiving you as being hard to work with—indecisive, reluctant to act independently, ingratiating, and relying excessively on others to make decisions.
- **Keeping Up with the Joneses**—In my executive coaching practice leaders will often compare themselves and their success (or lack of it) to others. This can be helpful in setting a benchmark,

but it rarely provides an accurate picture. When we look at our neighbors and their big house, big car, and big vacations, we're often unaware that this can equal big debt. When we make these comparisons at work, we can feel diminished and inferior. By all means be curious about others' career paths, their strengths at public speaking or negotiating, whatever it may be. But have a perspective that's empowering, asking yourself (and others) how you can grow. Comparing yourselves to others is a futile exercise, unless it inspires you to positive perception and positive action.

- **Habits and Behaviors**—We all have a track record of success, and a correlation between our "lucky socks" and the "outstanding presentation." However, we sometimes tend to overlook the fact that this success is because of habits that move us forward and also happens in spite of some behaviors. When we receive feedback from others that doesn't match our inside out view, we more easily dismiss it and choose not to act. Instead of ignoring feedback that doesn't match our self-image, we need to put ourselves in other people's shoes and remain curious; ask, "Why would someone think this about me?" This doesn't mean you have to act on all the feedback you receive, but you do need to hear it and recognize that at some point your inaction may limit the effectiveness of that relationship or your career.

- **Setting the Bar Too Low**—As humans, we seem to seek the path of least resistance in achieving goals—or we think small, embracing limiting beliefs about ourselves. Back in the early days of launching my company, I had a relatively small vision as to what I thought was possible; the size of organizations needing my expertise, the value I brought, and the fee I could command. Some of this was influenced by friends who had started their own businesses (keeping up with the Joneses) coupled with my own tendency to set the bar too low. Thankfully this mindset was quickly knocked out of me by mentors and other leaders who saw my potential. Even now, with an established track record, I still need reminding to set audacious goals.

- **Trash Talk**—We've already explored the impact of our internal voice, but trash-talk takes this to a whole new level. Here are some of the phrases we all need to remove from our lexicon.
  - o **"It was nothing."** Think about the last time you received a compliment. How did you respond? When we diminish our contribution it can be considered as humility, but at some point there is the risk that others will believe your PR (it really *was* nothing) and overlook the value you bring. When receiving a compliment or recognition for a job well done, try saying "Thank you" (even add some personal insight about why you enjoyed the project).
  - o **"I can't do that."** Remember the story about five-year-olds and painting? Children are novices at everything, yet that doesn't hold them back from trying—and learning. As adults, we don't like being seen as the novice, admitting we don't know something or how to do something. Yet every promotion, new job, new team, and new project brings change and the potential for being the novice. Being our own Ally allows us to admit to our hesitation and nerves and to take action in spite of them. Allies ask for help and take it when offered.
  - o **"That's not my job."** This mindset keeps you working within the parameters of your existing role and limits your opportunities to grow. If you are seeking a larger role or a more complex project, look for opportunities to develop your skills.

    I recall coaching a leader whose peer (described by her as an Ally) was encountering challenges with his team. Having listened to my client complain about her peer, I asked if she had offered to help. The answer was, "No, it's his boss's job to do that."

    In some ways, this leader was right, but she was also wrong. To be an Ally means you step in when others are in turmoil and offer support where you can. If you aspire to a higher leadership role, there will be times when you can step up and behave as a senior leader even if you don't have the title.

o **"I'm just a (insert job title)."** The word *just* is one of the most undermining words we can use. When I became a bank manager, I remember my cashiers, many of whom were part-time, describing themselves as "just a teller," playing down their roles within the branch and community. In my opinion, there was nothing *just* about being a teller. As the face of the bank, their positions were crucial. We worked together to change their false perception. This was not hype, a pep talk, or a slogan on a poster. We aligned their perception with the truth of their value within the organization. As a result, engagement increased, errors declined, customer satisfaction grew, and overall branch performance improved. I hope you'll have that same approach with yourself!

o **"It's not fair."** Growing up, I remember using this cry on a regular basis as I complained about my brother—we fought over who got the most soda, whose was the larger slice of pie, or whose turn it was to press the buttons in the elevator, and then we ran to our parents to complain that it "wasn't fair." We see this approach continue at work. Your colleague received a pay raise; you didn't. She got an award; you didn't. And "it's not fair." However, did you ask for the raise? Did you move out of your comfort zone and tackle a new challenge? Did you share your achievements (or acknowledge theirs)? This phrase doesn't move you forward, it keeps you trapped.

o **"I'll try."** As the wise sage Yoda said in *Star Wars*, "Do . . . or do not. There is no try." Saying "I'll try" implies you'll likely fail.

- **"He's an idiot (or other judgmental statement)."** Your words inform your emotions, which in turn drive behaviors. When you make negative judgments, you limit opportunities to respond positively to situations. This is why Communication forms an integral part of the Relationship Ecosystem™. Words matter, whether said out loud or as internal thoughts. Be aware of destructive language which damages relationships. Instead choose words that inspire and motivate you to take positive action with your colleagues.

• **Dwelling on past (or current) mistakes.** How much personal baggage are you carrying, with tags that read "I wish I'd . . ." or "I should have . . ." or "I could have . . ." Looking back at what could have been can be useful when it's a reflective part of a learning process. When it simply becomes a burden, this regret holds us back.

Don't Believe Everything You Think

We all have our own personal trash-talk phrases that crop up in our minds, and often at the most crucial moment:

• I am not talented enough (when waiting to follow another colleague who seems to deliver his or her presentation effortlessly).

• I missed that deadline again, therefore I am a failure.

• I can't volunteer to lead the new initiative, no one respects me enough.

• My creative solution to this problem will be shot down, so why bother?

Most of our thoughts are not a true picture of reality. And yet we often make our decisions based on a tightly held belief. These worries mask the truth about the opportunities in the here and now! Just because something *was* true doesn't mean it's true *now.* Just because something *might* happen doesn't mean it *will.* It might not be easy, but it's simple: you don't have to believe everything you think.

Changing Your Stories

Change your thoughts and you change your limitations. Change your thinking and you change the quality of your relationships. Start by deciding to be an Ally to yourself.

As I mentioned earlier, I used to be a couch potato. Finding the time to visit the gym on a regular basis didn't seem possible. However, looking back to my school life, I was a track athlete, regularly running 100 meters through 1500 meters. I even broke the school record for the 400 meters.

Yet my internal story was supported by so many phrases: "I am too busy," "I need to spend time with my family," "I don't like to get up early." These are essentially good reasons, yet they are simply excuses that were sabotaging me and my health. I was not being an Ally to myself.

Since the start of last year, I've recognized the irony of the self-inflicted behaviors and changed my story. I am now someone who exercises once a week. I am someone who has completed a sprint triathlon. I am someone who now aspires to visit the gym twice a week (my new threshold, which still triggers the excuses at even higher volume!).

I recall coming home from a busy day and asking my husband "Am I really a successful businesswoman?" I'm not sure what triggered the moment of self-doubt, but it was palpable. Even as I write this, many months later, there's a knot in my stomach. My husband, ever the pragmatist, responded with all the empathy he could muster: "If that wasn't the most ridiculous question I have ever heard, I would laugh!" Maybe it wasn't what I wanted to hear in that moment, but it certainly was what I needed to hear.

I recently stumbled across something I now call the "trash-talk rollercoaster." It goes something like this:

1. This is AWESOME!
2. This is harder than I expected.
3. This is awful!
4. I am awful.
5. This is barely OK.
6. This is AWESOME.

What I realized (and why I refer to this every day) is that this neatly summed up my thought process on a daily, hourly, minute-by-minute basis. And the really scary thing? It can take nano-seconds to go from number 1 to number 4. It can take considerably longer to get from 4 to 6 . . . without the help of an Ally.

Even after all this time living and relating these principles, debilitating moments of self-doubt can creep in. Being able to translate limiting self-talk into something more positive, being able to reach out to an Ally for an empathetic ear, or a quick kick in the pants, can be so critical.

What qualities make you successful? If you have recently taken a 360° feedback assessment, turn to the comments that showcase your talents and strengths. Reflect on them. Be proud of them. When you are having a bad day (and we all do) this is the time to return to these anchors, to remind ourselves that moments of weakness, moments of missed expectations, are just that—*moments*. These too will pass.

Hearing Voices

You have a choice: take on new challenges wholeheartedly, embracing the Ally voice (and learning from setbacks), or instead, cringe from the doubt that comes from Rival and Adversary voices. Learn to recognize the different voices, turn down the volume of your trash-talk, and practice acting as your own Ally.

Regularly ask for feedback—Feedback is designed to help you to overcome "in spite of" behaviors and reduce your blind spots. Most people who take the time to give feedback want to help you improve, not knock you down. However, in the moment it can feel like we are back in school being graded.

Feedback can be perceived as a threat by our reptile brain, resulting in a defensive reaction or ignoring the message because we don't respect the person who has delivered it. Because you want the best for your Ally (in this case, yourself) develop your emotional self-awareness so you can hear feedback from others. Ask clarifying questions if required. If you don't agree, thank the other person for her perspective and never tell her how wrong she is. (I'm joking. A little.)

Saying No—As an Ally to yourself, there will be times when you need to turn down opportunities and say no to requests. For those of us who value being helpful to others, this can be stressful and may result in the feeling that we are letting others down. Practice how you can say no while providing alternatives to others.

"I can't help right now as I need to focus on x, y, and z. However, I can dedicate time to this next week."

"I have other commitments this month, but perhaps we could meet next week so I can learn more about the project?"

Walk Your Own Path—Make your own choices when it comes to work, career, and family. Avoid deprioritizing your needs and desires in an attempt to live up to others' expectations. This only leads to frustration and disappointment. You (and I) already know this, but for some reason we need reminders. You get one go at this life: make it your own.

Take Baby Steps on Audacious Goals—If you were to coach a fellow Ally on your team, you'd want to give him every chance to succeed, right? So give yourself a break and give yourself the best chance to succeed. If you don't believe you can achieve a goal in one step, don't stop trying. Instead break it down into meaningful milestones that move you in the direction you want to go. Your confidence and sanity will increase as you go along.

So, are you an Ally to yourself? If you don't believe you are worthy of that level of relationship, how can you expect others to be your Ally? You can choose from three perspectives:

- The Ally perspective, which provides helpful insight into strengths and gaps.
- The Supporter perspective, which will highlight strengths but discount the weaknesses, those things you are successful in spite of.
- The Rival perspective, focusing only on the gaps and ignoring your strengths.

The last two choices are exhausting and full of disappointment, not just for you, but also for those who know you. Have you ever worked with a colleague who had obvious talents but didn't always bring them to the table? It's puzzling and frustrating. That's how other people see you when you diminish your contribution.

Adopting an Ally mindset toward yourself changes your thinking from "I can't because . . ." to a curious approach of "How can I?" A focus on "I can't because . . ." tends to trigger the limiting beliefs. A focus on curiosity and asking questions (out loud with an Ally, or in our heads) triggers the neocortex, the rational part of our brain that allows for complex thought, rational perspective, and most importantly, solutions, to help to move us forward. The options are unlimited when you are not limited.

When you are a true Ally to yourself, when you recognize that it's OK to be you, then you will find it easier to be an Ally to others, working alongside coworkers with compassion, respect, and without judgment.

RELATIONSHIP REVELATIONS

- It is imperative to be an Ally to yourself.
- Negative self-talk can be as debilitating as criticism from others.
- Develop the habit of reframing "I can't because . . ." into "How can I?"
- When we consider the Ally in the mirror, let's keep in mind the four questions below. You only have to think about all the self-made promises we break with ourselves—the diets or exercise plans we don't follow through on, or the promotions we don't apply for.
    1. Can I *count* on you?
    2. Can I *depend* on you?
    3. Do I *care* about you?
    4. Do I *trust* you?

YOUR RELATIONSHIP RESPONSIBILITIES

- What are two of your proudest career achievements?
- What future goals and dreams do you have?
    o What is the first step you can take to realize these?
    o Who can help you achieve this first step?
- To what extent are you an Ally to yourself?
    o What happens to your attitude and behaviors under pressure? Do you give up or do you stay in the game?
- What value do you contribute to your organization, your family, your community? (Not the role you fill, the value you contribute.)
    o Do you find yourself apologizing to others about things outside of your control?
- Write three positive statements about yourself that highlight your strengths.

CHAPTER 16

questions and conversation starters

The meeting of two personalities is like the contact of two chemical substances; if there is any reaction, both are transformed.

« CARL JUNG »

We've covered a lot of ground, exploring your Relationship Ecosystem™ and looking at new approaches for improving the health of your working relationships.

There's an old saying, "You can choose your friends, but you can't choose your family." It could as easily be, "You can choose your friends, but you can't choose your work colleagues." While you may not be able to choose your coworkers, you can now choose to:

- Identify your critical stakeholders on whom you are dependent for your success.
- Diagnose the quality of your working relationships and the context of each relationship.
- Identify the opportunities and actions to strengthen your working relationships.
- Identify the inherent risks of Rival, Supporter, and Adversary relationships.
- Deliver greater personal and team results by building Ally relationships.
- Share these concepts with your Allies and Allies-in-waiting.
- Connect and share your feedback with me!

Nobody can internalize all of this in one reading. That's why I've provided the recap below, and bonus resources online at www. CultivateTheBook.com. I also encourage you to keep this book handy and refer to it often.

Relationship Health Check Questions

Use these frequently to take a "pulse check" of the health of your working relationship.

- What has been happening for you since we last spoke?
- What's working well?
- What's getting in the way of our success?
- What have I done to amaze you recently?
- How have I missed expectations?
- What is one thing I can do to help ensure your/our success?

Alignment Questions and Tactics

- Rules of Engagement
  - When and how should we be collaborating?
  - What goals and priorities are of immediate importance to you right now? How are these (mis)aligned with my goals and priorities?
  - What is keeping you up at night?
  - How hands-on or hands-off would you like me to be?
- Understand Work Style: Consider using a psychometric tool such as MBTI or DISC to provide an understanding of the similarities and differences between you.
  - What do you do for fun outside of work?
  - What are your hot buttons? How will I know if you are stressed/frustrated?
  - Do you prefer phone, email or in person for our communications?
  - How often should we be meeting and for what purpose?
  - If I need your urgent attention, what should I say or do?
  - How can I best present bad news or tough messages in a way that you can hear and we can resolve together?
  - How would you describe your communication style? Are you direct, fact-based, logical, or more big-picture, options, and freewheeling?
  - Do you prefer to think things through or talk things out?
  - What is the biggest struggle you have had to overcome to get to where you are today?
  - What can I expect from you as a leader/colleague/ team member?
  - When do you do your best work?
  - What three adjectives would others use to describe you?
  - What three adjectives would you use to describe yourself?
- Agree on Decision Level and Approach
  - Which decisions do we each own?
  - How will decisions be made?
  - Who else needs to be involved and at what stage?
  - What problem-solving process will we use?
  - What are the inputs we are dependent on from others?

- o Who benefits from the outputs/work we create? In what format do they expect these?
- o Who has the information we need to inform our decisions?
- o Where do our roles and responsibilities stop and start?
- o When and how should we be collaborating?
- o What do you love about your job/role/organization?
- o What keeps you here?
- o What might cause you to leave?
- o What roadblocks are you experiencing?

Adjustment Questions
- Baggage Questions
  - o In what ways have I missed expectations?
  - o In what ways do I act inconsistently with our rules of engagement?
  - o What bugs you about my working style?
  - o What do I need to know that we haven't discussed previously?
  - o What is getting in the way of my success?
- The Apology
  - o What do I need to apologize for?
- Forgiveness
  - o What do I need to forgive?
- Name the Elephant
  - o What are the issues that we should be discussing, but aren't?
  - o What issues persist because we are not discussing them?
  - o What is preventing us from raising these topics?
  - o How is this impacting us personally or professionally?
  - o What price are we paying for our silence?
  - o What organizational barriers are making it hard for us to work effectively together?
  - o What interpersonal dynamics are making it hard for us to work effectively together?
  - o What is one thing I could do differently that would make life easier?

Adjust Questions
- Feedback
  - What is my reputation? What do others see or say?
  - What are my blindspots?
  - What do I need to know that would help our/my effectiveness?
  - What is one strength I could continue to leverage or develop?
  - When have I missed your expectations?
- Course Correct
  - What am I working on that is not value added?
  - What do I do that interferes with the quality of our relationship?
  - Does our relationship feel out of balance?
  - What is one piece of advice you have for me/my team?
  - Goodbye

Applaud Questions
- Thank you
  - How do you like to give/receive recognition?
  - What do you like to be recognized for?
  - What contributions do you like to be valued for?
  - What impact have you had in my success? Be specific in your thanks!
- I am your Ally
  - "My number one job is to ensure your success."
- Celebrate Success
  - What can we learn from this?
  - How can we incorporate this going forward?
  - What is the biggest struggle you have had to overcome to get to where you are today?

Endnotes

1 Daniel Goleman, *Working with Emotional Intelligence* (New York: Bantam, 1998).
2 http://www.astd.org/Publications/Magazines/TD/TD-Archive/2012/11/ ASTD-2012-State-of-the-Industry-Report.
3 John Kotter, "What Effective General Managers Really Do," *Harvard Business Review*, March 1999.
4 Lynda Gratton and Tamara Erickson, "Eight ways to build collaborative teams," *Harvard Business Review*, November 2007.
5 Michael Watkins, *The First 90 Days*, (Harvard Business Review Press, 2003).
6 Janet Kornblum, *USA Today*, June 2006, http://usatoday30.usatoday.com/news/ nation/2006-06-22-friendship_x.htm; accessed November 2013.
7 Stephen Adams, *The Telegraph*, January 2012, http://www.telegraph.co.uk/tech-nology/news/9033161/Facebook-friends-cant-be-relied-on-in-a-crisis.html; accessed April 2013.
8 "The relationship between engagement at work and organizational outcomes." 2012 Q12™ meta-analysis, Gallup Organization, February 2013.
9 Tom Rath, *Vital Friends—The People You Can't Afford to Live Without* (New York: Gallup Press, 2006).
10 Dunbar, Robin I.M., *How Many Friends Does One Person Need? Dunbar's Number and Other Evolutionary Quirks* (London: Faber and Faber, 2010).
11 Forbes.com, December 19, 2012, http://www.forbes.com/sites/susan-adams/2012/12/19/why-gossip-is-good-for-the-office/, accessed July 2, 2013.

Bring *Cultivate* to your organization

Keynote

Cultivating winning relationships is powerful when you have a group or organization all working as a team of Allies.

Contact us today to explore how we can help you leverage the power of *Cultivate* across your organization. Email us at info@skyeteam.com or call 1-303-800-5442.

Keynote Speaking

Morag Barrett and her team are regularly invited to speak at conferences, leadership events, and at company meetings. Whether you have a team of 10 or 500+ leaders you can expect a powerful, culture-shifting message.

Enjoy fast-paced, entertaining, and interactive sessions at your next corporate or association event. Morag customizes her keynotes, seminars, and workshops to support your event theme. Because she invests time getting to know you, your organization, and event participants, you'll experience a custom learning event that exceeds expectations. Your attendees will engage, and more importantly, leave with tools they can apply immediately to have a positive impact on their success, and the success of those around them.

When you work with Morag you can expect:

- A discovery meeting to learn about your organization, and to discuss the goals for your event.
- A highly engaging session that will ensure your participants can articulate why quality working relationships matter to the business—and their personal impact. They will apply The Relationship Ecosystem™ to identify the actions needed to develop Ally Relationships.
- A post-event meeting to review feedback and provide recommendations to maintain momentum.

In addition to *Cultivate: The Power of Winning Relationships*, Morag delivers keynote topics that make the challenges of leadership, management, and human resources pragmatic and fun!

WORKSHOP

"Difficult to manage relationships sabotage more business than anything else."—JOHN KOTTER, HARVARD BUSINESS SCHOOL.

Cultivate is available as a powerful workshop experience, *"Cultivating Winning Relationships."* Experienced SkyeTeam facilitators will partner with you throughout the planning process to ensure that the workshop supports your strategic priorities.

There is also the option to license the content for delivery by your in-house facilitators. SkyeTeam provides an intensive *train-the-trainer* experience to prepare your delivery teams to provide the workshop to your employees.

Participant benefits
- Articulate why quality working relationships matter: the business and personal impact.
- Apply the Relationship Ecosystem™ to diagnose the health of professional relationships.
- Determine the next steps to develop Ally relationships and manage Adversary relationships.

Target Audience
- Association Conferences and Meetings
- Cross Functional Teamwork Programs
- Executive Development Programs
- High-Potential Leadership Programs
- Leadership Retreats or Summits
- Leaders and employees at all levels

Options
- ½ day workshop
- 1-day workshop
- 2-day workshop
- Custom Programs
- Train-The-Trainer

KEYNOTE AND WORKSHOP
TESTIMONIALS

"Cultivate is what I have been waiting for, I just didn't know it. The workshop was fun, engaging and left me with a plan of action that I will implement immediately."

"This is an excellent program. I am going to recommend this, and the book, to everyone I know."

"Thank you for sharing your experience and expertise. The workshop helped me to realize that I need to spend more time on cultivating winning relationships. My success depends on it!"

Contact us today to explore how we can help you leverage the power of Cultivate across your organization. Email us at info@skyeteam.com or call 1-303-800-5442.

SkyeTeam.com
People. Leadership. Results.

At SkyeTeam we know that your company is unique. Your culture is your own, and your people are unlike any others. We don't bring preconceived solutions to your company, we listen. We take the time to learn about you, your business, and your employees to deliver the most effective Human Resources solutions.

How do we do it? First, we work closely with you to understand your strategic business goals, as well as your company's language and culture. We need to grasp a comprehensive understanding of who we are helping; Is it the organization as a whole, your team, or an individual? Only then do we make an informed recommendation that will deliver an immediate return on investment.

SkyeTeam's leadership and management development programs, executive coaching, and team development events will help you keep your cool when the heat's on.

We specialize in high impact
- Executive coaching and new leader on-boarding,
- Executive retreats and meeting facilitation,
- High performing team development,
- Human Resources consulting, and
- Leadership and management development programs.

Contact us today to explore how a partnership with SkyeTeam could transform your results info@skyeteam.com

www.skyeteam.com/services

people. leadership. results.

About The Author

Morag Barrett is a leadership development expert, speaker, author, and founder of SkyeTeam. She is dedicated to helping individuals, teams, and organizations achieve extraordinary business results through effective leadership development and human resources management.

Prior to founding SkyeTeam, Morag held leadership positions at Level 3 Communications, and NatWest Bank where she advised international organizations on their corporate strategy and growth plans. Originally from the UK, she has experience with a wide range of cultures and businesses, and has developed high potential individuals and teams across the United States, Europe, and Asia. Morag brings more than 25 years of industry experience and a deep understanding of the complexities of running a business and leading executive teams.

Morag has worked with over 3,000 executives and senior leaders in FTSE 100 and Fortune 100 organizations in more than twenty countries including National Westminster Bank, Newmont Mining, Western Union, Great West Financial, Level 3 Communications, Clearwire, DexMedia, and Scholastic.

Morag is regularly invited to speak at industry, organization, and association events and is a guest lecturer at the University of Denver. Her expertise has been highlighted through her contributions to *TheStreet. com*, *Inc.com*, American Management Association (AMA), American Society for Training and Development (ASTD), the Society for Human Resource Management (SHRM) and the National Business Education Forum. In addition to *Cultivate*, she has published articles for *T&D* Magazine and the American Management Association.

Morag Barrett has a Masters in Human Resource Management, is a Chartered Fellow of the Chartered Institute of Personnel and Development, and a certified business coach.

Morag has established herself very happily in Broomfield, Colorado, with her husband and three sons. For fun, in addition to time with her family, you'll find Morag playing in the Broomfield Symphony Orchestra, where she is the principal bassoonist and member of the board. She also loves ocean sailing and ballroom dancing. In case you're wondering, her name is Scottish and means "great."

www.SkyeTeam.com

www.MoragBarrett.com

morag barrett
BUSINESS IS PERSONAL